1974

WHAT A YEAR TO BE BORN!

Written by
Robin Bennett-Freebairn and Joe Toussaint

Published by Emersive
www.whatayeartobeborn.com

What happened in 1974? Most of us have a special affinity for the year we were born, but how much do we really know about it? This guide takes you through the highs and lows of an historic year in the middle of Generation X. The colour-coded chapters unlock a wealth of information, bringing you closer to what life was like in this special year.

Contents

▶ Introduction

On New Year's Day much of Britain had a lie in. A new public holiday was declared across the nation (Scotland had been taking this day off since 1871.) London enjoyed a crisp, clear day, New York was covered in snow and in Sydney they headed for the beach. 1974 was a year of huge political and social turmoil. January 1st was the first day of the three-day week in the UK. It was brought about by a combination of the oil crisis stemming from the Arab-Israeli Yom Kippur War and strikes by the miners' union, the NUM. In February, Conservative Prime Minister Edward Heath went to the country, asking the electorate: "Who Rules Britain?" The answer came back "Not you"; the Labour Party of Harold Wilson won with a small majority. In America, the Watergate scandal finally caught up with President Richard Nixon and he resigned. Vice President Gerald Ford was sworn in after a vote in Congress. He immediately pardoned Nixon. When he lost the 1976 election to Jimmy Carter, he became the only US President in history never to have been directly elected.

It was a year of disappearances. When MP John Stonehouse's clothes were found on a Miami Beach he was presumed dead, only to turn up in Australia some months later. One person who would not reappear, although there were numerous alleged sightings, was Lord Lucan. He disappeared into thin air after the shocking murder of his children's nanny.

It was a good year in the field of entertainment. Disaster movies were popular and the star-studded *The Towering Inferno* had audiences on the edge of their seats. At the Oscars, *The Sting* starring Paul Newman and Robert Redford scooped the award for Best Picture.

ABBA won the Eurovision Song Contest with their song *Waterloo* and what is considered to be the first 'Stadium Rock' concert was fronted by the band Yes, at Madison Square Garden, New York City.

In sport, West Germany won the football World Cup and in boxing, huge underdog Muhammed Ali defeated the all conquering George Foreman, in what was billed as "The Rumble in the Jungle". In racing the legendary Red Rum won his record-breaking third Grand National and in cricket, Lillee and Thompson let rip during a successful Ashes series for Australia. In domestic football, Leeds United won their second title. Afterwards their manager Don Revie took over the England job from Alf Ramsey, who was sacked after the national team failed to qualify for the World Cup.

The most popular girls' names of the year were Sarah and Claire. For boys it was Paul and David. The year saw the invention of the Rubik's cube, brainchild of Hungarian architect Erno Rubik. It has 43 quintillion combinations. The world record for solving it is currently held by 'supercuber' Max Park in 3.13 seconds.

The Daily Headlines

No: 8706

Price: Three pence

Evening Edition

Wednesday, March 20, 1974

ATTEMPTED KIDNAP OF PRINCESS ANNE AT GUNPOINT IS FOILED BY BRAVE PASSER-BY

The Daily Headlines

Price: Three pence

Friday, August 9, 1974

No: 10214

Evening Edition

PRESIDENT NIXON RESIGNS FROM OFFICE AS A CONSEQUENCE OF THE WATERGATE SCANDAL

The Daily Headlines

Price: Three pence

Tuesday, October 10, 1974

No: 10272

Evening Edition

HAROLD WILSON WINS A THREE SEAT MAJORITY FOR LABOUR IN CLOSE FOUGHT GENERAL ELECTION

The Daily Headlines

No: 10301

Evening Edition

Price: Three pence

Friday, November 8, 1974

BRITISH PEER LORD LUCAN VANISHES INTO THIN AIR AFTER NANNY FOUND MURDERED IN HIS LONDON HOME

Jan 1st	Across the UK many people enjoy a lie in, as New Year's Day is declared a public holiday nationwide for the first time. (Residents in Scotland have enjoyed the paid holiday for nearly a century.) For many it is the first of numerous days off as a fuel crisis has forced the government to declare a 3-day working week. Many jobs hang in the balance.
Jan 2nd	In order to preserve oil stocks, US President Nixon signs an order reducing the speed limit on roads from 70mph to 50mph.
Jan 2nd	Cracks are beginning to show aboard the US spacecraft Skylab 4, although thankfully not to the ship itself. During a live broadcast astronaut William Pogue declares himself to be a fallible human being, while mission commander Gerald Carr says he misses a cold beer.
Jan 4th	Citing executive privilege, President Nixon refuses to hand over 500 documents relating to the Watergate investigation.
Jan 11th	The first surviving sextuplets are born to 25-year-old Susan Rosenkowitz in Cape Town, South Africa.
Jan 12th	When Manchester United visit West Ham, George Best's name is not on the team sheet. The off-field antics of the greatest home grown footballer of his generation have become too much for manager Tommy Docherty, so he is kicked out of the club.
Jan 15th	Comet Kohoutek makes its closest approach to Earth, passing at 0.8 astronomical units. Don't worry, that's about 74 million miles and it is just about visible to the naked eye.
Jan 18th	Israel and Egypt sign an agreement ending the Yom Kippur war on the Egyptian front.
Jan 20th	For the first time in England, a professional soccer game is played on a Sunday. Held at Millwall, the hosts defeat Fulham 1-0. The goal is scored by Brian Clarke after four minutes.
Jan 23rd	Ewch â fi at eich arweinydd (that's "take me to your leader" in Welsh). Lights and noises are heard on the Berwyn Mountains in North Wales.

Many people believe it to be a UFO landing. Scientists say that it is caused by the combination of an earth tremor and a meteor.

Jan 24th — Colour television comes to New Zealand in time for the Commonwealth Games, which are opened by Prince Philip in Christchurch.

Jan 25th — Yale University declares that the Vinland map, which purportedly shows a portion of North America explored by Lief Eriksson in the 11th century, is a 20th century forgery.

Feb 4th — The National Union of Miners call an all-out strike to begin in 5 days' time.

Feb 4th — In the US, the left-wing terrorist group The Symbionese Liberation Army kidnap Patty Hearst from her apartment in Berkeley, California. She is the granddaughter of newspaper magnate W. Randolph Hearst.

Feb 7th — Prime Minister Edward Heath goes to the Queen to ask for the dissolution of Parliament, precipitating a general election.

Feb 12th — Peter Firmin and Oliver Postgate's stop-motion, animated, stuffed cloth cat *Bagpuss* makes his television debut.

Feb 13th — Russian historian and novelist Aleksandr Solzhenitsyn is deported from the Soviet Union to Frankfurt, West Germany.

Feb 20th — Cher files for separation from her husband Sonny Bono.

Feb 21st — Tim Horton, Canadian ice hockey legend and co-founder of the Tim Hortons restaurant chain, is killed in a car accident in Ontario, Canada.

Feb 23rd — A World War I artillery shell explodes in Italy killing seven people. They had been exploring the site of the 1916 Battle of Asiago.

Feb 28th — Voters across the UK go to the polls in what is expected to be a close contest between the ruling Conservatives and the Labour opposition. Opinion polls have the Conservatives two points ahead.

Mar 1st — As the results of the general election come in, it is clear there is going to be

a hung Parliament. Labour secure 301 seats and the Conservatives 297. The Liberals hold the balance of power with 14 seats; scant reward for their 19% share of the vote.

Mar 3rd   After taking off from Orly Airport in France bound for London, Turkish airlines Flight 981 suffers catastrophic explosive decompression. All 346 passengers and crew are killed.

Mar 4th   Harold Wilson stands on the steps of Number Ten Downing Street as he becomes Prime Minister for the second time. He tells the assembled press and public "We've got a job to do. We can only do that job as one people and I'm going right in to do that job now".

Mar 7th   The striking miners are awarded a 34% pay rise. The 3-day week and state of emergency that had been in place since New Year's Day are cancelled.

Mar 7th   Miss World, American Marjorie Wallace, is sacked for bringing the pageant into disrepute by having 'multiple celebrity boyfriends'.

Mar 20th   Ian Bell, a man with acute mental health problems, attempts to kidnap the Queen's daughter, Princess Anne, at gunpoint. After shooting four people, including Anne's bodyguard, passer-by and ex-boxer Ron Russell punches Bell and leads Anne to safety.

Mar 23rd   604 speakers are lined up at Cow Palace near San Francisco at a gig held by the Grateful Dead in what was known as the "Wall of Sound" concert.

Mar 29th   The Terracotta Army of Qin Shi Huang is discovered by farmers at Xi'an, China.

Mar 30th   Red Rum wins back-to-back Grand National steeplechases.

Mar 31st   British Airways is created after the merger of British European Airways, British Overseas Airways Corporation and a few smaller companies.

Apr 1st   Residents of Sitka, Alaska wake to see smoke billowing from nearby Mount Edgecumbe, a volcano that had been dormant for 400 years. However, the volcano was not about to blow. The smoke was the work of

local prankster Oliver 'Porky' Bickar, who set fire to dozens of tyres on top of the volcano. Most people eventually saw the funny side.

Apr 2nd At the 46th Academy Awards, Glenda Jackson wins Best Actress for her role in *A Touch of Class*, while Jack Lemmon is deemed Best Actor for *Save the Tiger*. The event is interrupted by a male streaker and host David Niven quips: "Isn't it fascinating that probably the only laugh this man will get in his life is by stripping off and showing his shortcomings."

Apr 3rd The largest tornado outbreak in history hits southern parts of the Ohio and Tennessee Valleys. More than 100 recorded tornadoes leave 335 people dead, causing $600 million of damage in their wake.

Apr 5th Garfield Sobers and Rohan Kanhai play their last test match for the West Indies cricket team.

Apr 7th Just in time for Easter, Kinder Surprise chocolate eggs hit the shelves.

Apr 10th Magicians Penn Jillette and Teller first meet.

Apr 15th Ireland's Neil Cusack wins the men's race at the 78th Boston Marathon in a time of 2h 13m. American Miki Gorman wins the women's race, clocking 2h 47m.

Apr 29th President Nixon says he will release partial transcripts of the Watergate tape recordings.

May 1st Following their failure to qualify for the World Cup, England sack their manager Alf Ramsey.

May 4th An all-female Japanese group of climbers reach the summit of Mount Manasalu in the Himalayas; the first women to climb a peak of over 26,000ft.

May 6th West German Chancellor Willy Brandt resigns over an aide's links to the East German security service, the Stasi.

May 8th The largest walkout in history takes place when 1.2 Million railway and ancillary workers go on strike in India.

May 9th   The US House of Representatives Judiciary Committee begins formal hearings on President Nixon's impeachment for events surrounding the Watergate Scandal.

May 17th   German footballer Franz Beckenbauer lifts the European Cup as his Bayern Munich team beat Athletico Madrid 4-0 in the final in Brussels.

May 18th   India becomes the sixth nuclear power when it tests a weapon in Rajasthan. They join the US, the Soviet Union, the United Kingdom, France and China at the top table of destruction.

May 24th   David Bowie releases his eighth studio album, *Diamond Dogs*, which was recorded in London and the Netherlands.

May 26th   Around 800, mainly girls and young women, are injured during a crush at pop idol's David Cassidy concert in London. 14 are seriously injured.

May 27th   A boat capsizes on the Parana River in Brazil. The waters are infested with piranhas. Only one of the 14 people on board survives.

May 27th   More than 12,000 people attend the funeral of jazz legend Duke Ellington at the Cathedral of St. John the Divine in New York. Attendees include Ella Fitzgerald, Earl Hines and Count Basie.

May 28th   Johnny Carson hosts the 26th Emmy Awards at the Pantages Theatre, Los Angeles. British drama *Upstairs, Downstairs* wins the award for Outstanding Drama Series. Alan Alda and Mary Tyler Moore win Best Actor and Best Actress respectively.

Jun 1st   It is now safer not to chew when eating, as thoracic surgeon Henry Heimlich publishes a paper detailing a method for dislodging food from the windpipe. The Heimlich Manoeuvre immediately catches on among servers across America, ensuring that diners make it through to settle the bill and leave a tip.

Jun 1st   At The Flixborough chemical plant in Lincolnshire the largest ever peacetime explosion in Britain occurs. The blast causes a blaze that rages for 16 days and leaves 28 workers dead and a further 56 injured.

 **News Journal**

Jun 4ᵗʰ   It comes as no surprise that the '10c Beer Night' promotion at the Cleveland Stadium, between the home team the Indians and the visiting Texas Rangers, descends into violence. No limits are placed on the amount of alcohol consumed. The teams have to use their bats to defend themselves after a pitch invasion.

Jun 8ᵗʰ   Jon Pertwee makes his last appearance as Dr. Who. Tom Baker becomes the new incarnation along with a much longer scarf.

Jun 11ᵗʰ   A young law professor by the name of Bill Clinton becomes Democratic nominee for the Representative of the Third District of Arkansas.

Jun 15ᵗʰ   Carl Bernstein and Bob Woodward's *All the President's Men*, exposing the Watergate investigation, is published.

Jun 16ᵗʰ   Björn Borg wins the French Open tennis tournament coming from two sets down to beat Manuel Orantes of Spain, in spite of wearing shorts that seem far too tight!

Jun 24ᵗʰ   Casual dining chain Spudulike opens its first outlet in Edinburgh. There is a choice of toppings ranging from tuna mayonnaise, to cheese, to beef chilli. All the better after a night in the pub.

Jun 26ᵗʰ   After ten years of marriage, Elizabeth Taylor and Richard Burton divorce.

Jul 1ˢᵗ   In Argentina, upon the death of her husband Juan Perón, deputy President Isabel Perón becomes the first woman to rise to be the President of a nation.

Jul 6ᵗʰ   At the Wimbledon Final, Jimmy Connors defeats Ken Rosewall in straight sets; the day after his fiancée Chris Evert defeats Olga Morozova.

Jul 7ᵗʰ   West Germany's Gerd Müller scores the winner as the host nation defeat The Netherlands in the FIFA World Cup final.

Jul 13ᵗʰ   South African Gary Player wins the Open Golf tournament at Royal Lytham & St.Annes. He leads in all four rounds, finishing four shots ahead of Britain's Peter Oosterhuis.

Jul 25ᵗʰ   War is over. The Cod War that is. The World Court rule in favour of the UK and West Germany in a fishing dispute with Iceland. It is decided that Iceland cannot extend its fishing limits from 12 miles to 50 miles.

Jul 28ᵗʰ   The Campaign for Real Ale withdraw their guide 'Avoid At All Costs' for fear of being sued by British breweries.

Aug 7ᵗʰ   In a carefully planned operation, French daredevil Philippe Petit and friends link the twin towers of the World Trade Center in New York with a high wire. He then traverses the gap eight times waving, kneeling and even dancing above a growing crowd of onlookers.

Aug 9ᵗʰ   On White House notepaper a letter signed by Richard Nixon reads "I hereby resign the Office of President of The United States". It is witnessed by Secretary of State Henry A. Kissinger. Vice President Gerald Ford is sworn in as the 38ᵗʰ President of The United States of America.

Aug 14ᵗʰ   The collapse of the package holiday company Court Line leaves 50,000 British holiday makers stranded overseas. Some are being turned away from hotels, others have to sleep on the floor.

Aug 16ᵗʰ   In reaction to Court Line's failure the government, aided by other travel companies begins the biggest repatriation of its citizens from mainland Europe since the evacuation of Dunkirk during World War Two.

Sep 8ᵗʰ   A month into his presidency, Gerald Ford pardons former President Nixon. The pardon is wide-reaching and absolves Nixon of "any crimes he may have committed against the United States as President".

Sep 9ᵗʰ   Scottish strongman Bill Anderson wins his sixteenth consecutive Highland Games Championships.

Sep 13ᵗʰ   Two adolescent pandas, Chia Chia and Ching Ching are flown to London to be housed at London Zoo after being gifted by China. The pandas' dietary needs are very particular and they each require half a ton of bamboo every week. The rest of the time they spend sleeping.

Sep 13ᵗʰ   NBC in America go big in the battle for Friday ratings when they launch

The Rockford Files, starring James Garner and *Police Woman* with Angie Dickinson. CBS hit back with *Planet of the Apes* starring Roddy McDowall.

Sep 17th Originating in America in 1965, Bold detergent comes to the UK. It is marketed as Britain's first low suds, biological detergent.

Sep 18th Just a stone's throw from where the Titanic was built, a 348ft crane called Samson is built at the Harland and Wolff shipyard in Belfast. It now sits alongside the smaller, 315ft tall Goliath, that was built in 1969.

Oct 1st "Make mine a Baileys". Named after a restaurant in Ireland, the iconic whiskey, cream and herb liqueur is introduced to the market.

Oct 3rd 39-year-old Frank Robinson becomes Major League Baseball's first African-American manager when he signs a one-year contract to become player-manager of the Cleveland Indians.

Oct 5th Dave Kunst becomes the first person to walk around the world on foot when he arrives back home in Waseca, Minnesota. He has walked nearly 9,000 miles. He set off with his brother John in June 1970, but John was murdered in Afghanistan in 1972.

Oct 5th A bomb, believed to be the work of the Irish Republican Army, explodes in the Horse and Groom public house in Guildford, killing five and injuring 54. A second device in the city's Seven Stars explodes after the pub had been evacuated so there are no fatalities.

Oct 8th Welsh language soap opera *Pobol y Cwm* (English: *People of the Valley*) is broadcast on BBC Cymru for the first time.

Oct 9th Czech born industrialist Oskar Schindler dies. Originally a Nazi supporter, he then risked his life to save over 1,200 mainly Jewish people from near certain death during World War II.

Oct 10th For the first time since 1910, two general elections are held in the same year in the UK. The Labour Party, led by Harold Wilson, secures a small majority. It was business as usual for former Scottish Nationalist MP Robert McIntyre as he lost in his ninth attempt to return to the house.

Oct 12th   Arnold Schwarzenegger scoops the top prize of $1,000 in a run off against Lou Ferrigno at the Mr. Olympia bodybuilding contest held at Madison Square Garden, New York.

Oct 21st   If you can understand the rules you are smarter than me! The first modern role-playing game (RPG) *Dungeons and Dragons* is released. 1,000 sets are produced by American publisher Wizards of the Coast and are targeted at college students who should be submitting their dissertations.

Oct 30th   In Kinshasa, Zaire, the 'Rumble in the Jungle' boxing match between champion George Foreman and Muhammed Ali ends in victory for Ali when he knocks Foreman out in the 8th round.

Nov 8th   British peer, Lord Lucan, disappears into thin air after his children's nanny is found murdered in London.

Nov 11th   Operatic soprano Maria Callas announces that her appearance in Sapporo, Japan is to be her last.

Nov 12th   A salmon is discovered in the River Thames for the first time since 1833. (and no, it wasn't in a tin)

Nov 13th   It's "hold the onions, extra pickles, hold the lettuce, extra mayo and double cheese please", as McDonald's opens its first UK restaurant in Woolwich, South East London. A hamburger cost a mere 15p.

Nov 16th   On the back of their Eurovision Song Contest victory, Swedish pop sensations ABBA embark on their first overseas tour.

Nov 18th   *The Lamb Lies Down on Broadway* album by prog-rock band Genesis is released as front man Peter Gabriel announces that he is leaving the group.

Nov 20th   The clothes of MP John Stonehouse are found on a beach in Florida. It is assumed he has drowned.

Nov 21st   Two bombs, planted by the Irish Republican Army explode in packed Birmingham pubs, killing 21 people and injuring 220.

Nov 23rd African National Congress activist Thabo Mbeki marries social worker Zanele Dlamini, in a ceremony in London.

Nov 29th A special service for the recently deceased Nicolai Poliakoff, aka Coco the Clown, is held at St. Paul's Cathedral.

Dec 4th French philosopher Jean-Paul Sartre visits Baader-Meinhof leader Andreas Baader in prison in Germany.

Dec 5th The final episode of *Monty Python's Flying Circus* airs on BBC television.

Dec 10th The Nobel Peace Price is shared between Irishman Seán MacBride for his work on human rights and Japanese Prime Minister Eisaku Satō for his commitment to nuclear non-proliferation.

Dec 14th Isaac Vivian Alexander 'Viv' Richards scores his first test century when he amasses a total of 192 runs against India.

Dec 17th Mud's *Lonely This Christmas* reaches No.1 in the UK pop charts. And yes, it is supposed to sound like Elvis.

Dec 18th Japanese soldier Terou Nakamura, declared dead in 1944, emerges from the jungles of Indonesia. For almost thirty years he believed that the Pacific war was still raging. He is the last known Japanese soldier to formally surrender.

Dec 22nd The Provisional IRA bomb the home of former Prime Minister Edward Heath, before announcing a Christmas ceasefire.

Dec 24th MP John Stonehouse is arrested in Melbourne. He had faked his own death to escape fraud charges in the UK.

Dec 25th The city of Darwin in Northern Australia is overwhelmed by a cyclone producing winds of up to 135 mph. Many of the city's buildings cannot withstand the storm leading to considerable damage and loss of life.

Dec 31st The Ballon D'or, recognising the best European footballer of the year, is awarded to Dutchman Johan Cruff. West Germany's Franz Beckenbauer comes second.

 ## Melanie Jayne Chisholm aka **Mel C**
born on 12th January 1974 in Whiston, Merseyside, UK

After school, Mel studied for a diploma course in singing, dancing and musical theatre at the Doreen Bird College of Performing Arts in London. It was there she replied to an advert in *The Stage*, placed by a producer who was looking to form a girl band. Around 400 women answered the advert. Geri Halliwell, Mel, Victoria Adams and Melanie Brown were originally chosen for the band, later forming a quintet with Emma Bunton. Of all the women who became the Spice Girls, Mel C is the most successful. On top of the 100 million records she sold with the band she has sold over 23 million as a solo artist. In 1997, she had a brief relationship with Robbie Williams. She later had a long term relationship with property developer Thomas Starr, with whom she had a daughter, Scarlet. The two separated in 2012. Outside of her career as a performer, Mel C has appeared as a judge and mentor in reality competition talent shows like *Asia's Got Talent*, *The X Factor Australia* and *Superstar*. In 2019, she reunited with her Spice Girl band mates (except Victoria Beckham) for their *Spice World* tour. On the 15th September 2022, she released her memoir *Who I am : My Story*.

Mel, dubbed Sporty Spice, was the member of the band who most lived up to their epithet, although with the concession that Ginger (Geri Halliwell) was ginger for a time. Mel has competed in several races including the London Triathlon and the 2016 Blenheim Palace Triathlon and her *Rock Me* was chosen as the anthem for the 2011 FIFA Women's World Cup.

 ## Katherine Ann Moss
born on 16th January 1974 in Croydon, London, UK

Kate Moss is a British supermodel renowned for her iconic presence in the fashion industry. Moss catapulted to fame in the early 1990s, heralding the era of 'heroin chic' with her waifish figure and distinctive features. Moss's career breakthrough came at the age of 14 when she was discovered by Sarah Doukas, founder of Storm Model Management, at JFK Airport in New York City. Her unconventional beauty challenged traditional standards; she quickly became a muse for renowned designers such as Calvin Klein and Gianni Versace. Throughout her illustrious career, Moss has graced countless magazine covers, walked prestigious runways and starred in numerous high-profile advertising campaigns. Her influence extends beyond modelling; she has collaborated with major brands like Topshop and launched her own successful fragrance lines. Despite occasional controversies and setbacks, including public scrutiny of her personal life, Moss's career has endured, and she remains a leading figure in the fashion world. Her signature style and effortless cool continue to inspire designers and photographers worldwide. Beyond her professional achievements, Moss's enduring appeal lies in her ability to reinvent herself while maintaining an enigmatic allure. Her legacy as a cultural icon transcends generations, cementing her status as one of the most influential models of all time.

In 2008 Marc Quinn made a 50kg, 18-carat gold statue of Moss entitled *Siren* for a British Museum exhibition. It is said to be the largest gold statue to be created since Ancient Egypt.

 ### Christian Charles Philip Bale
born on 30th January 1974 in Haverfordwest, Wales, UK

Bale's rise to fame was stellar. In 1983, he appeared in a cereal commercial. Later that same year he made his West End Debut in Larry Shue's play *The Nerd*. When he appeared in the US miniseries *Anastasia: The Mystery of Anna*, he caught the eye of Steven Spielberg who cast him in *Empire of the Sun* (1987), for which he won a young actors' award. Bale then appeared in Kenneth Branagh's 1989 adaption of Shakespeare's *Henry V*. By the 1990s, he was appearing on our screens regularly in such movies as *Newsies* (1992), *Little Women* (1994) and *Metroland* (1997). In 2000, he landed the role that took his fame to another level, when he played a murderous Wall Street executive in *American Psycho*. The new century saw him display his vast acting range with starring roles in *Shaft* (2000), *Captain Corelli's Mandolin* (2001) and *Laurel Canyon* (2002). Bale's ability to immerse himself into a character led Christopher Nolan to cast him in *Batman Begins* (2005), the first of a trilogy with a dark narrative. Bale would follow up playing Bruce Wayne/Batman in *The Dark Knight* (2008) and *The Dark Knight Rises* (2012). In 2011, he won a best supporting actor Oscar for his role in *The Fighter*. Bale is known for his incredible ability to change his physical body shape whether gaining or losing weight to realistically inhabit the characters he portrays.

If he plays an American character, he will use an American accent in all the interviews promoting the film. He says he does this so the audience is not confused.

 ### Sarah Caroline Sinclair aka Olivia Colman
born on 30th January 1974 in Norwich, Norfolk, UK

Olivia Colman is a highly acclaimed British actor known for her versatility, emotional depth and captivating performances across film, television and theatre, She initially gained recognition for her work in British comedy, before transitioning to more dramatic roles. Colman's breakthrough came with her role as Sophie Chapman in the popular British comedy series *Peep Show* (2003-2015), where she showcased her comedic talents alongside David Mitchell and Robert Webb. However, it was her poignant portrayal of complex characters in dramas that truly solidified her reputation as one of Britain's finest actresses. One of Colman's most notable performances came in the critically acclaimed film *The Favourite* (2018), directed by Yorgos Lanthimos. Her portrayal earned her widespread acclaim and the Academy Award for Best Actress, catapulting her to international stardom. In addition to her film work, she has made a significant impact on television. She delivered a memorable performance as Detective Sergeant Ellie Miller in the crime drama series *Broadchurch* (2013-2017), further showcasing her range as an actress. Colman's talent extends to the stage as well, with notable performances in productions such as *The Threepenny Opera* and *Hay Fever*, earning her critical acclaim and several award nominations.

Olivia became one of only six actors to have portrayed two Queens on screen. She played Elizabeth II in *The Crown* (2020) and Queen Anne in *The Favourite* (2018). The others are Cate Blanchett, Helena Bonham Carter, Bette Davis, Judi Dench and Helen Mirren.

Robert Peter 'Robbie' Williams
born on 13th February 1974 in Stoke-on-Trent, Staffordshire, UK

Robbie Williams is a British singer-songwriter who rose to prominence as a member of the boy band Take That in the 1990s before embarking on a highly successful solo career. He demonstrated his musical talents from a young age, but it was his audition for Take That in 1990 that launched his career into the spotlight. With the band, Williams achieved massive commercial success, contributing to hit singles like *Back for Good* and *Never Forget*. However, his tenure with the group was marked by personal struggles, including battles with substance abuse and mental health issues. In 1995, he left Take That to pursue a solo career. Williams' career skyrocketed with the release of his debut album, *Life thru a Lens*, in 1997, which featured the hit single *Angels*. He followed this success with numerous chart-topping albums, including *I've Been Expecting You* (1998), *Sing When You're Winning* (2000) and *Escapology* (2002). Known for his charismatic stage presence, cheeky personality and powerful voice, Williams became one of the best-selling music artists globally. His eclectic blend of pop, rock and swing influences have contributed to his broad appeal. Beyond his music career Williams has had the odd foray into acting, featuring in *Gangsta Granny* (2013) alongside Julia McKenzie and Joanna Lumley.

In January 2024, Port Vale football club appointed life-long fan Williams as their life president. Williams was pleased, stating "My life is bizarre... to find myself from the Railway Paddock to be 'El Presidente' is pretty special".

James Hillier Blount aka James Blunt
born on 22nd February 1974 in Tidworth, Hampshire, UK

James Blunt is an English singer-songwriter known for his emotive voice and poignant lyrics. Blunt pursued a career in music after serving in the British Army. He gained widespread recognition with his debut album, *Back to Bedlam*, released in 2004. The album's lead single, *You're Beautiful*, became an international sensation, propelling Blunt to global fame. Blunt's music is characterised by its heartfelt themes of love, loss and introspection, often accompanied by his distinctive raspy voice and acoustic guitar melodies. His songwriting style is deeply personal, drawing from his own experiences and emotions. Despite occasional criticism for his melancholic lyrics, his sincerity and authenticity have endeared him to audiences worldwide. Over the years, Blunt has released several successful albums, including *All the Lost Souls* (2007), *Some Kind of Trouble* (2010) and *Moon Landing* (2013). His music spans various genres, incorporating elements of pop, rock and folk, while maintaining a consistent introspective tone. In addition to his musical endeavours, Blunt has also been involved in philanthropic work, supporting causes such as environmental conservation and veteran support initiatives. Aside from his music career, he is known for his wit, often displayed through his social media posts. He engages with fans candidly, displaying a down-to-earth personality that contrasts with the melancholy of his music.

From Twitter (now X). Follower: James Blunt looks like a serial murderer. James Blunt's response: I know where you live.

Victoria Caroline Beckham OBE
born on 17th April 1974 in Harlow, Essex, UK

Born Victoria Caroline Adams, she rose to fame in the 1990s as 'Posh Spice' in the iconic British girl group, the Spice Girls. While the group achieved global stardom with hits like *Wannabe* and *Spice Up Your Life*, her influence transcended her role in the band. After the Spice Girls broke up in 2000, she pursued a solo music career but, meeting only limited success, she eventually shifted her focus to fashion. She launched her eponymous label in 2008. She quickly gained recognition for her sophisticated and minimalist designs, earning praise from critics and celebrities alike. Beckham's impact on the fashion world extends beyond her own brand. She has collaborated with renowned designers, including Estée Lauder, further solidifying her status in the fashion business. Victoria Beckham is also known for her high-profile marriage to former professional footballer David Beckham. The couple, often referred to as 'Posh and Becks', have become synonymous with modern celebrity culture and are one of the most recognisable A-List couples worldwide. Despite her success, Victoria has often faced scrutiny and criticism throughout her career, particularly regarding her weight and public persona. However, she has consistently demonstrated resilience and determination, using her platform to advocate for body positivity and women's empowerment. In recent years, she has expanded her business empire, branching out into skincare, fragrance and a lifestyle brand.

She earned the nickname 'Posh' after her dad used to drop her off at school in his swanky Rolls Royce.

Penélope Cruz Sánchez
born on 28th April 1974 in Alcobendas, Madrid, Spain

Penélope Cruz is a celebrated actress known for her versatility. From her early days in Spanish cinema to international acclaim, she has solidified her status as one of the most respected actresses of her generation. Cruz's career began in the early 1990s with her breakout role in 1992 in Bigas Luna's Spanish romantic comedy *Jamon Jamon* (literally Ham, Ham) where her performance earned her worldwide attention. She continued to rise in prominence with roles in films like *Open Your Eyes* and *The Girl of Your Dreams*, earning several Goya Award nominations. In 2001, Cruz made her mark in Hollywood with roles in films such as *Vanilla Sky* alongside Tom Cruise and *Blow* with Johnny Depp. Cruz continued to enthral audiences with her performances in films like *Volver*, for which she received an Academy Award nomination for Best Actress, making her the first Spanish actress to achieve this honour. Throughout her career, Cruz has showcased her versatility by portraying a wide range of characters in various genres, from drama to comedy. Her collaborations with acclaimed directors like Pedro Almodóvar and Ridley Scott have further showcased her exceptional talent and versatility. In 2018 she won a Prime Time Emmy Award for her portrayal of Donatella Versace in the miniseries: *The Assassination of Gianni Versace: American Crime Story*.

Her sister Monica was used as a body double during the filming of *Pirates of the Caribbean: On Stranger Tides* (2011) on account of Cruz being seven months pregnant.

Sir Anthony Peter 'AP' McCoy OBE
born on 4th May 1974 in County Antrim, Northern Ireland

Sir Anthony Peter McCoy, commonly known as Tony McCoy or simply AP McCoy, is a legendary Northern Irish jockey renowned for his extraordinary achievements and dominance in the world of horse racing. McCoy began his career as a jockey at the age of 17. He moved to England in 1994 and served as conditional jump jockey to Toby Balding, being crowned champion conditional in 1995. McCoy's career spanned over two decades during which he amassed a record-breaking number of wins, making him one of the most successful jockeys in the history of the sport. His unprecedented 4,358 career wins surpassed the previous record held by Richard Dunwoody. Throughout his career, McCoy clinched virtually every major title and accolade in horse racing, including an incredible 20 consecutive Champion Jockey titles in the UK, a feat unparalleled in the sport's history. He has won many prestigious races such as the Grand National, Cheltenham Gold Cup, Champion Hurdle and King George VI Chase. McCoy's relentless work ethic, determination and unparalleled talent made him a box office favourite to race goers. During his career he broke nearly every bone in his body from his cheekbone to his ankle; he gained a reputation as something of an iron man when it came to recovering from serious injury.

Tony's best friend is the other great jockey of recent years, Rupert 'Ruby' Walsh. Walsh, who rode primarily in Ireland, would pop over to England most weekends to ride and spent the nights at McCoy's house in Lambourn. He even had his own bedroom called 'Ruby's Room'.

Image: © The Jo Cox Foundation

Helen Joanne 'Jo' Cox
born on 22nd June 1974 in Batley, West Yorkshire, UK

Jo Cox was a passionate campaigner, activist and humanitarian; a proud Yorkshire lass and internationalist, a devoted mum, daughter, sister, wife and friend. She was driven by her belief that a fairer, kinder and more tolerant world was possible and dedicated her career to helping those less fortunate than herself. Jo lived by the words she expressed in her first speech in Parliament: "We are far more united and have far more in common than that which divides us". Jo became the first member of her family to go to university, gaining a place at Pembroke College, Cambridge. After graduating, she headed off to Borneo for three months to work on conservation projects. Jo fought passionately for the rights of women and children, directing the Maternal Mortality Campaign with Sarah Brown at the White Ribbon Alliance. She also worked for organisations including Save the Children and the NSPCC. In early 2015, Jo heard that the current MP for Batley and Spen was retiring and she seized the opportunity to stand as the Labour candidate and become the local MP. On 16th June 2016, on her way to a constituency surgery, Jo was murdered because of her beliefs. In her short-time in parliament, Jo made a huge impact and gained respect across the house.

Inspired by Jo, her family and friends set up The Jo Cox Foundation. The charity channels the energy and determination generated by Jo's life and tragic death into practical efforts to make change on the issues that she was passionate about.

Maxine Peake
born on 14th July 1974 in Bolton, Greater Manchester, UK

Peake is a highly acclaimed British actor known for her versatile performances across stage, television and film. Her career has spanned over two decades, marked by her exceptional talent and dedication to her craft. Peake first gained recognition for her role as dappy Twinkle in the television series *Dinnerladies* (1998-2000), created by Victoria Wood. Her breakthrough came with her portrayal of Veronica Ball in the gritty drama series *Shameless* (2004-2007), where she showcased her ability to inhabit complex characters with depth and authenticity. In addition to her television work, she has made significant contributions to the stage. She has performed with theatre companies such as the Royal Shakespeare Company and the Royal Exchange Theatre, earning critical acclaim for her roles in productions like *Hamlet* and Lillian Hellman's *The Children's Hour*. Peake's filmography boasts a diverse range of roles, including historical dramas like *The Theory of Everything* (2014), where she played the wife of Stephen Hawking and contemporary dramas like *Funny Cow* (2017), in which she starred as a stand-up comedian navigating the male-dominated world of comedy. Beyond her acting, Peake is admired for her outspokenness on social and political issues. She has been an advocate for various causes, including gender equality and workers' rights, using her platform to raise awareness and effect change. In 2020, she appeared as Mrs Fozzard in Alan Bennett's reprise of his *Talking Heads* Series.

As a teenager Maxine played rugby league for her local Wigan women's team.

Timothy Henry Henman OBE
born on 6th September 1974 in Aston Tirrold, Oxfordshire, UK

Tim Henman, a former professional tennis player from Great Britain, made a significant impact on the sport during his career. He became one of the most successful British tennis players of his generation. His playing style was characterised by his serve-and-volley approach, excellent net play and a strong baseline game. He possessed a formidable forehand and a reliable backhand slice, which he used to great effect throughout his career. One of Henman's career highlights was reaching the semifinals of Wimbledon four times, in 1998, 1999, 2001 and 2002. His performances at the All England Club earned him the nickname 'Tiger Tim' and made him a fan favourite. Although he never won a Grand Slam singles title, he claimed 11 ATP singles titles and reached a career-high ranking of world number 4 in 2002. He also achieved success in doubles, winning six ATP doubles titles during his career. His contributions to British tennis extended beyond his on-court achievements. He played a key role in inspiring a new generation of players and raising the profile of tennis in the United Kingdom. After retiring from professional tennis in 2007, Henman has remained involved in the sport as a commentator and tennis pundit. The viewing screen at Wimbledon, perched on top of a mound, is informally known as 'Henman Hill' in Tim's honour.

Henman's achievements on the tennis court have often been underrated. It should be remembered that he won six out of the first seven matches he played against Roger Federer.

Gok Wan MBE
born on 9th September 1974 in Leicester, Leicestershire, UK

Gok Wan is a British fashion consultant, television presenter and author known for his expertise in style, body positivity and confidence-building.. Much of his passionate campaigning stems from the fact that he was bullied when younger for being both overweight (he states that he weighed 21 stone at one point) and gay. Wan rose to prominence in the mid-2000s with his television series *How to Look Good Naked*. The show revolutionised the way people perceived fashion by promoting self-acceptance and celebrating diverse body types. With his infectious personality and keen eye for fashion, he became a household name, known for his catchphrases and empowering messages. He encouraged viewers to embrace their bodies, regardless of size or shape, and offered practical styling advice to boost self-esteem. In addition to his television career, Wan has authored several books, including *How to Dress: Your Complete Style Guide for Every Occasion* and *Gok's Wok*, showcasing his passion for both fashion and food. He has also collaborated with major retailers, designing clothing lines aimed at promoting body confidence and inclusivity. In 2017, he released an opera compilation CD, *Gok's Divas*, which reached number one in the classical music charts. He is also an accomplished DJ and has toured Europe playing his favourite house music.

In June 2023, Wan played a set at the Glastonbury Festival in front of 100,000 adoring fans.

Leonardo Wilhelm DiCaprio
born on 11th November 1974 in Los Angeles, California, USA

DiCaprio is one of Hollywood's most famed and versatile actors. He first came to public attention in *This Boy's Life* (1993) where he played a teenager oppressed by his father. Later that year in *What's Eating Gilbert Grape*, he filled the role of an altogether different character when he played a young man with learning difficulties. He gained widespread recognition for his role as Jack Dawson in James Cameron's epic romance *Titanic* (1997), which became the highest-grossing film of its time. However, it was his collaboration with director Martin Scorsese that solidified his status as a powerhouse actor. Films like *Gangs of New York* (2002), *The Aviator* (2004), *The Departed* (2006), *Shutter Island* (2010) and *The Wolf of Wall Street* (2013). These films showcased his exceptional range and garnered him multiple award nominations, including several Academy Award nominations. Beyond his collaborations with Scorsese, DiCaprio has demonstrated his versatility in various genres, from drama to thriller to biopic. He delivered compelling performances in *Catch Me If You Can* (2002), *Inception* (2010), *Django Unchained* (2012) and *The Revenant* (2015), the latter earning him his first Academy Award for Best Actor after several nominations. Apart from his acting prowess, DiCaprio is known for his environmental activism.

When DiCaprio, director James Cameron and co-star Kate Winslet, heard that Millvina Dean, the last survivor of the sinking of the Titanic, was forced to sell her mementos to pay for her care, they contributed $50,000 towards a fund in her name.

 ## Paul Scholes
born on 16th November 1974 in Salford, Greater Manchester, UK

Scholes is a retired English footballer widely regarded as one of the greatest midfielders of his generation. He spent the entirety of his professional career at Manchester United, becoming one of the club's most decorated players. Renowned for his exceptional vision, passing ability and knack for scoring crucial goals, Scholes made his debut for Manchester United in 1994 and quickly established himself as a key player under manager Sir Alex Ferguson. His technical proficiency, intelligent movement and precise long-range shooting earned him admiration from fans and peers alike. During his illustrious career, he won numerous honours, including eleven Premier League titles (only Ryan Giggs with 13 has more), three FA Cups and two UEFA Champions League titles. He also represented England at international level, earning 66 caps and scoring 14 goals. Despite his modest demeanour off the field, Scholes commanded respect on it, becoming a linchpin in United's midfield for over two decades. His playing style was characterised by crisp passing, impeccable ball control and an innate understanding of the game's nuances. He retired from professional football in 2013, leaving behind a legacy as one of United's greatest ever players. Beyond his playing career, Scholes has remained involved in football as a pundit and occasional coach.

When the great Zinadine Zidane was asked which player he would have liked to have played with he answered, without hesitation, Paul Scholes.

 ## Other Notable Births

Matt Lucas 5th March 1974 Actor | Comedian	**Vaughan Gething** 15th March 1974 Politician	**Adil Ray** OBE 26th April 1974 Actor | Comedian
Andrea Corr 17th May 1974 Singer | Songwriter	**Denise van Outen** 27th May 1974 Actor | Presenter	**Alanis Morrisette** 1st June 1974 Singer | Songwriter
Kelly Jones 3rd June 1974 Singer | Musician	**Bear Grylls** 7th June 1974 Adventurer	**David Mitchell** 14th July 1974 Actor | Comedian
Hannah Waddingham 28th July 1974 Actor | Presenter	**Jimmy Fallon** 19th September 1974 TV Host | Comedian	**Matthew Macfadyen** 17th October 1974 Actor
Joaquin Phoenix 28th October 1974 Actor	**Stephen Merchant** 24th November 1974 Actor | Comedian	**Sara Cox** 13th December 1974 Broadcaster | Author

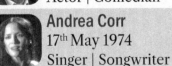 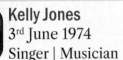 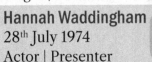 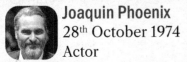

H. E. Bates CBE
died aged 68 on 29th January 1974 in Canterbury, Kent, UK

Herbert Ernest Bates, commonly known as H.E. Bates, was a prolific English writer born in 1905. Renowned for his evocative prose and keen observation of rural life, Bates captured the essence of the English countryside in his works. His writings often delved into themes of nature, love and the human condition, drawing inspiration from his upbringing in Northamptonshire. He gained widespread acclaim for his short stories, such as those in *The Darling Buds of May* series, which portrayed rural life with warmth and humour. Additionally, he wrote novels like *Fair Stood the Wind for France* and *Love for Lydia*, showcasing his versatility as a writer. David Jason and Pam Ferris played Pop and Ma Larkin in a TV adaptation of *The Darling Buds of May* (ITV 1991-3). The show also featured a young Catherine Zeta-Jones. *Fair Stood the Wind for France* was made into a miniseries in 1980 and starred Cécile Paoli and Eileen Way.

Edward Kennedy 'Duke' Ellington
died aged 75 on 24th May 1974 in New York City, USA

Duke Ellington was a towering figure in American music, particularly jazz. Renowned as a composer, bandleader and pianist, his career spanned over five decades. His innovative compositions, characterised by rich harmonies and sophisticated orchestrations, revolutionised jazz and influenced countless musicians. His orchestra, known as the Duke Ellington Orchestra, became legendary for its tight arrangements and virtuosic performances, featuring iconic soloists such as saxophonist Johnny Hodges and trumpeter Cootie Williams. Throughout his career, Ellington composed an extensive repertoire, including timeless classics like *Take the A Train*, *Mood Indigo* and *Sophisticated Lady*. His music transcended racial barriers, earning him widespread acclaim and recognition as one of the greatest composers of the 20th century. Beyond his musical contributions, Ellington was a cultural ambassador, touring extensively worldwide and representing the best of American music.

Georgy Konstantinovich Zhukov
died aged 77 on 18th June 1974 in Moscow, Soviet Union

"Where Zhukov goes we go, when Khokov is there we win." That was the mantra of the Red Army and they were right. Zhukov was the most important general in the European theatre during the Second World War. But it was only by chance that he survived Stalin's purge of the army in the 1930s. He slept with a packed suitcase and revolver for much of his life in case 'Uncle Joe's' henchmen came a-calling. Zhukov played a pivotal part in several decisive battles, including the defence of Moscow, the Battle of Stalingrad and the successful operation to lift the Siege of Leningrad. His most notable achievement was the commanding role he played in the Battle of Berlin, leading to the final defeat of Nazi Germany. In the victory parade in Moscow, Stalin was scheduled to ride a white horse, but it bolted and unseated the dictator during rehearsals. Stalin, jealous of the adulation afforded to Zhukov, ordered the general to ride the feisty horse. He did it with aplomb, much to Stalin's chagrin.

Lyudmila Mikhailovna Pavlichenko
died aged 58 on 10th October 1974 in Moscow, Soviet Union

Lyudmila Pavlichenko, born in 1916, was a Soviet sniper during World War II, hailed as one of the most successful snipers in history. Growing up in Ukraine, she displayed a passion for shooting from a young age. When Germany invaded the Soviet Union, she volunteered for the Red Army and quickly proved her marksmanship skills. During the war she recorded 309 confirmed kills, including 36 enemy snipers, making her an icon of Soviet resistance. Her bravery earned her numerous accolades, including the Order of Lenin. Pavlichenko also became the first Soviet citizen to be received by a US President when she visited Franklin D. Roosevelt. Her visits to the United States and Canada helped rally support for the Allied cause. After the war, she pursued a career in academia, advocating for the rights of veterans and women in the military. Lyudmila Pavlichenko's legacy remains an inspiring testament to courage, skill and resilience in the face of adversity.

Karen Gay Silkwood
died aged 28 on 13th November 1974 near Crescent, Oklahoma, USA

Karen Silkwood was an American chemical technician and labour activist known for exposing safety violations at the Kerr-McGee plutonium plant where she worked. In the 1970s she became increasingly concerned about the health and safety risks posed by the plant's operations, particularly the lack of proper safety measures and the mishandling of plutonium. She began collecting evidence of these violations to present to the Atomic Energy Commission. However, before she could do so, Silkwood died in mysterious circumstances in a car accident. Many believe she was deliberately silenced to prevent her from exposing further wrongdoings. Her death led to a significant legal battle and public outcry, shedding light on the dangers faced by workers in the nuclear industry and inspired increased protection for whistle-blowers. In 1983, Meryl Streep starred in a film based on the book, *Who Killed Karen Silkwood?*, by Howard Kohn.

Jack Benny born Benjamin Kubelsky
died aged 80 on 26th December 1974 in Los Angeles, California, USA

Jack Benny was a funny man who could arrive on stage, violin in hand and have the audience in stitches even before he spoke. Born Benjamin Kubelsky in 1894, he was a legendary American comedian, known for his impeccable timing and dry humour. Rising to fame in vaudeville, Benny transitioned to radio in the 1930s with *The Jack Benny Program*, captivating audiences for over 20 years. His radio show featured characters like Rochester, his sharp witted butler and Benny's own tight-fisted persona that became his trademark. In the 1950s, he took his show to television and his relaxed demeanour attracted guests like Marilyn Monroe and Humphrey Bogart, stars who rarely appeared on the small screen. Benny's enduring legacy was his work for civil rights. He would frequently have guests like Louis Armstrong and The Ink Spots on his show. Rochester, his fictional valet and friend in real life, was the highest paid African-American actor in the 1950s.

The average salary in the UK in 1974 was around:

£2100 per year

equivalent to £40 per week

The price of the average house would be approximately 5x the average annual salary. Depending on where you were in the country this meant the price of a typical 1970's 3-bedroom semi-detached house would be in the region of:

£9,000 – £10,000

The Mark III Ford Cortina was launched in the UK in 1970. In 1972, it became the UK's best selling car; a position it would retain until 1976. It was available in 4 trim levels: Base, L (luxury), XL (Xtra Luxury), GT (Grand Touring) and GXL (Grand Xtra Luxury - pictured). In 1974, a basic Ford Cortina 1300L cost:

£1,150.00

A Sony Trinitron colour television set cost:

£175.00

In 1974, a pint of milk cost:

5 pence

A gallon of petrol (which equates to 4.5 litres) cost:

38 pence

School in the 1970s

The huge upheaval in state education in the UK that started in the 1960s continued in the 1970s. In 1970, 62% of state school pupils were educated in the tripartite (grammar/technical/secondary modern) system and 31% in comprehensive schools. By the end of the decade, 89% of state school pupils went to comprehensives. Politicians still debated the merits of the two systems, but time was up for most of the grammars. There was change in primary education as well. The middle school system, where children were educated at middle schools up to age twelve or thirteen, was introduced by many local authorities. Infants and juniors became first and middle schools. Pupils took GCE (General

An art class in 1974

Certificate of Education at Ordinary (O-level) or Advanced (A-level)) and/or CSE (Certificate of Secondary Education). In 1975, a grading system was introduced for O-levels. Grades A-C were equivalent to the former GCE O-level pass. School started at age five in the 1970s. Children started school at the beginning of the term in which they had their fifth birthday. They were usually aged four when they first entered the school gates. The school leaving age at the start of the 1970s was fifteen. It was raised to sixteen in 1972. Children were able to leave in the term following their fifteenth or sixteenth birthday. Those old enough were known as 'Easter leavers'. Even after the increase in school leaving age 'Easter leavers' left school with no qualifications. In the 1970s there were primary and secondary schools as there are today. The age range at primary school was five to between eleven and thirteen, and at secondary school up to eighteen. Some primary schools were organised into infants and juniors, as they were in the 1950s and 1960s. Middle schools could educate pupils up to age thirteen before transfer to secondary schools. By the end of the 1970s about 20% of pupils at age eleven went to middle schools. The remainder were educated in a system that allowed transfer to the secondary school at age eleven. Most would have taken some examinations, either GCE O-levels or CSEs (from 1965). Some stayed on at school after sixteen to study GCE A-levels. Selection at age eleven was disappearing in the

Chess clubs in schools were popular in 1974 following Bobby Fischer's epic win against Boris Spassky two years earlier

1970s. For many children there was relief at not having to take the dreaded Eleven-plus. For others, there was disappointment at a missed opportunity. Those who had good grades in their A-levels had the chance to go to university. The number who chose to had risen from one in twenty five to one in seven by the 1970s. For those who missed out, the Open University was a godsend. Much as it does today, it offered adults a route back into further education. It awarded its first degrees in January 1973.

School Type	1970	1975	1980
Secondary Modern	41%	19%	6%
Grammar	20%	10%	4%
Technical College	2%	1%	<0.5%
Comprehensive	31%	68%	91%
Other (mainly private)	7%	3%	5%

The change in UK school types over the decade

Background

The Eleven-plus exam, introduced in 1944 by the Education Act in the UK, is an entrance examination taken by students at the age of 11. The purpose of the exam is to determine their academic ability to govern admission to grammar schools and other secondary schools which use academic selection. Students who perform well in the exam are selected for grammar schools, offering an academic curriculum, while those with lower scores attended secondary modern schools or technical schools, offering a more vocational education. The Eleven-plus exam played a significant role in the education system until its gradual phasing out in the 1970s due to criticisms of its inequality. However, it is still used to this day in some schools.

Here's your chance to test yourself with example questions from the 1970s:
(Answers on page 92)

Arithmetic Questions

Question One: A train leaves London at 10:30am and arrives at Birmingham at 12:40pm. It stopped from 12:10pm to 12:20pm at Coventry which is 100 miles from London. It travelled both parts of the journey at the same rate. Find the distance from London to Birmingham.

Question Two: If 1st December falls on a Monday, on what day will Christmas Day fall that year?

Question Three: A machine makes toy soldiers at the rate of 75 in 5 minutes. How long with it take to make 6,000 of them? (answer in hours and minutes)

Question Four: Write in figures the sum of four hundred and forty six and seventy-seven.

Question Five: John is 12 years old and his mother is 42. Answer the following:

A) How old was John's mother when she was 4 times as old as him?

B) In how many years' time will his mother be three times as old as John?

C) How old will John be when his mother is 10 times as old as he was 6 years ago?

General English Questions

Question One: Change all necessary words to make these sentences plural:

A) My dog is carrying a stick.

B) His butcher has no meat.

C) A man who likes football is sure to have a team scarf in his house.

Question Two: Fill in the blank with a suitable missing word:

A) As *toe* is to *foot* so is .... to *hand*.

B) As *referee* is to *football* so is .... to *tennis*

C) As *Spain* is to .... so is *France* to *Frenchmen*

Question Three: Rewrite each of these sentences replacing the underlined words with a single word:

A) I was <u>in no doubt</u> that the shop would be closed.

B) He said that he would be coming home <u>in a short time</u>.

C) She <u>made up her mind</u> to go the cinema.

Top 10 Girls' Baby Names [1]

1. **Sarah** — of Hebrew origin meaning 'princess'
2. **Claire** — from the French for 'clear' in its feminine form
3. **Nicola** — from the Greek god of victory Nike
4. **Emma** — from Old German meaning 'universal' or 'whole'
5. **Lisa** — a shortening of the Hebrew *Elisheba* meaning 'God is my oath'
6. **Joanne** — of French origin meaning 'God is gracious'
7. **Michelle** — of Hebrew and French origin meaning 'who is like God'
8. **Helen** — possibly from the Greek *Selene* meaning 'Moon'
9. **Samantha** — possibly a compound of *Samuel* 'name of God' and *Anthea* 'flower'
10. **Karen** — a Danish derivative of Katherine meaning 'pure'

Top 10 Boys' Baby Names [2]

1. **Paul** — from Latin meaning 'Small' or 'Humble'
2. **David** — corruption of the Hebrew name *Dawid* meaning 'beloved'
3. **Mark** — from the Latin name Mart-kos 'consecrated to the god Mars'
4. **Andrew** — of Greek origin meaning 'Garland or crown'
5. **Richard** — from Old German meaning 'Powerful leader'
6. **Christopher** — a biblical name meaning 'Christ-bearer'
7. **James** — originates from the Hebrew name Ya'aqov meaning supplanter
8. **Simon** — from Hebrew meaning 'he his heard'
9. **Michael** — of Hebrew origin meaning 'One who is like God'
10. **Matthew** — from Greek via Hebrew meaning 'gift of God'

[1] [2] Data compiled by the Office for National Statistics 1974

Games, Toys and Pastimes

Collecting trading card stickers was a popular pastime for kids in the '70s. The Italian company Panini published its first FIFA World Cup sticker album in 1970 for the World Cup in Mexico. In the early '70s, Clackers were one of the first 'fads' that took the playground by storm. By spinning the two solid plastic balls connected by string they made a distinctive clacking sound. However, they tended to shatter, so were soon banned. Space Hoppers were advertised as 'the amazing inflatable riding ball'; everyone wanted one. However, most of us discovered that skinned knees came as part of the bargain! If you didn't own a View-Master in the '70s, you probably knew someone who did. With just a click on the dial, you could scroll through images of faraway places or gaze at pictures of popular TV shows. The roller-skating trend has been coming and going since the '60s, but the arrival of disco music in the '70s made it popular with both young children in the playground and teenagers on the dance floor of the nearest roller disco. Other popular toys included Meccano, Subbuteo, Barbie dolls, Chopper bikes, Action Man, the Fisher Price Chatter Telephone, Crossfire Rapid-Fire Game, Spirograph, Lego and Etch-A-Sketch.

Clackers

Space Hopper

The Life of a Coal Miner in the 1970s

In the 1970s, coal miners in Great Britain were skilled technicians, far removed from the stereotypical image of manual labour with picks and shovels. Before descending into the mine, they changed into their working clothes leaving their regular clothes in a locker on the clean side of the pit head baths. They also collected their cap lamps and self-rescuers, a visual sign of the industry's commitment to safety. On their way to the pit head, miners would pass the giant powerhouse which provided power to the sophisticated mining machines, the shaft lifts and windings and the enormous fans which provided the forced underground ventilation. In this mechanised environment, miners were provided with comprehensive training. They became all-rounders, skilled in various tasks throughout the mine. Despite the perception of mining as hazardous, safety was a top priority with miners adhering to a strict underground code to protect themselves and their fellow workers. This fostered legendary collaboration and team spirit. The main roadways leading away from the pit-bottom were spacious passageways,

Checking the tungsten teeth

Operating the cutting machinery at the coal face

connecting to subsidiary roadways and ultimately leading to the coal faces. These roadways, reinforced with steel arches, facilitated the movement of men and materials to the coal face whilst speedily transporting the coal away from it. Approaching the coal face, miners would pass under massive steel hydraulic supports capable of bearing the enormous loads on the tunnel walls. The coal-cutting machine, armed with tungsten steel teeth, extracted up to 375 tonnes of coal in a single cut. The extracted coal was automatically fed onto conveyors, efficiently transporting it to through the shafts and to the surface, all the while being sprayed with water to minimise airborne coal dust. The 1970's mine incorporated comprehensive medical facilities, ensuring the miners' health and well-being. Each colliery had a fully-equipped Medical Centre, run by either a qualified Nursing Sister or trained medical attendants. After their shifts, miners cleaned up in the pithead baths, emerging refreshed and clean. The nearby canteen provided a selection of snacks for the miners on their way to or from work. Despite the challenging conditions underground, miners worked with advanced machinery and received excellent medical support. Mining played a vital role in powering the nation and stood as a testament to human adaptability and resilience.

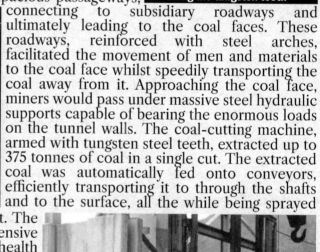

Miners returning to the surface after a shift

The Life of a Telephonist

By the 1970s, large swathes of British industry were under state control. One such job in a state run industry was that of a telephonist. In the early 1970s, telecommunications were still under the control of the General Post Office (GPO). No formal qualifications were required to become a telephonist, although a test which consisted of spelling UK place names and basic numeracy had to be passed. If accepted for the job, basic training was given, which usually consisted of shadowing an experienced telephonist. As the GPO was part of the civil service, the Official Secrets Act had to be signed, although quite what secrets a telephonist might be privy to one can only imagine. Also, men were required to wear a tie, even though no member of the public would ever see them. The equipment in most exchanges was little changed since the Second World War. The telephonist would sit in front of a switchboard, wait for a light to flash, insert a jack into a socket and say the words "Operator services, how may I help you?" The calls could vary from asking for a dialling code, checking why a number was engaged, checking why a line was dead or placing a call overseas to a place without direct dialling. The job was relaxed and fun and quite frankly overstaffed. Direct dialling, which had been rolled out since 1958, meant that the workload of the telephonist was a fraction of what it had previously been, although staffing levels remained high.

Exchange equipment was used for decades

Industrial Relations

Between the 1950s and the 1970s, the two main political parties each had periods in office, but the coal, energy, rail and telecommunications industries remained in public ownership. By and large the Labour party were more enthusiastic about nationalisation, even proposing that the sugar and cement industries were brought under state control. However, this did not materialise. In the early 1970s, British Leyland, a car manufacturer, was nationalised by the Conservative government of Edward Heath under the guise of a rescue package. Until the arrival of the Thatcher government at the end of the decade, the status quo of state ownership remained. This had consequences for both major political parties, as these industries were heavily unionised. Trade Union leaders could deliver a 'bloc vote' at the Trade Union Congress (TUC) or through their funding of the Labour Party at their annual party conference. The raising of an arm by a union boss, could represent hundreds of thousands of votes. There was always much talk of "beer and sandwiches at Number 10" as union leaders sought to influence government policy. It also meant that the government, as the de facto employer of so many people, was responsible for negotiations over pay and conditions. The squeeze on oil production in the Middle East, in retaliation for the West's support for Israel in the Yom Kippur War (October 1973) put further strain on industrial relations and emboldened the National Mineworkers' Union (NUM) to demand more money as coal was needed to keep the country going. On 1st May 1973, over one and a half million workers went on strike in a show of solidarity and industrial strife would eventually bring down the Conservative government of Edward Heath.

Interior design trends in 1974 saw vibrant colours reflecting the optimism and energy of the time, as well as the influence of psychedelic and pop art movements. Patterns and prints were also widely used, incorporating geometric shapes and bold floral designs. Earthy tones and textures, such as terracotta and jute, were embraced to create a warm and inviting atmosphere. This bedroom has a typical patterned wallpaper. Notice also, the designer bedside table.

A picture of the author's family gathered in the lounge for a photo. The room is dominated by the brightly patterned chairs and sofa.

Carpet in the bathroom became very popular in the early 1970s. Coloured three-piece bathroom suites also became the height of fashion. Matching textile bathmats and toilets seat covers completed the look.

A design trend in the early 1970s, which became popular for those who could afford it, was the sunken lounge. Creating a lowered area to enclose the seating along with a fire or wood burning stove was a place for relaxation and conversation. This particular room is from a house in Australia.

The kitchen of 1974 also had a colourful makeover including coloured worktops, a patterned linoleum floor and matching wallpaper. Light fittings, curtains and an oil skin tablecloth complete the look for this particular contemporary kitchen.

Actor Peter Sellers is photographed in his mews home in Belgravia, London. This image with its portable TV, portable radios and LP records stacked under the table demonstrates how technology was starting to dominate the layout of living rooms.

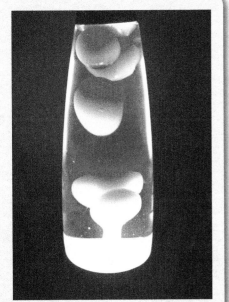

Invented 10 years earlier, lava lamps were a popular feature in British living rooms along with bean bags and wicker furniture.

Thick carpets with a deep pile made of the shag fabric were very popular in the 1970s. The carpet shown here has a classic colour combination mixing the two popular colours of avocado and harvest gold. Not so easy to vacuum!

Macramé wall hangings and plant hangers were popular in 1974. The intricate woven designs created from knotted cords added a bohemian and handmade touch to the decor. Macramé was also used to decorate shelf edges.

Chilli con carne might seem a little mundane these days, but in the early to mid seventies it first came onto the scene and made a big impact with Brits who were more used to spuds than spice. This classic combination of minced beef and kidney beans has been a treasured recipe ever since. The origins of the dish can be traced back to Mexico. In writings from 1529, the Franciscan friar Bernardino de Sahagún described chilli pepper seasoned stews being eaten in the Aztec capital Tenochtitlan, now in modern-day Mexico. Its first appearance in a recipe book came in the US in the 1850s. The less than appetising recipe involves dried beef, suet, dried chilli peppers and salt, which were pounded together, formed into bricks and left to dry. The would then be boiled in a pot and served.

In the 1970s it quickly caught on as a cheap and cheerful meal, particularly among students and young people. Many people, usually men would claim to cook a "mean chilli" and would also claim to have a secret recipe. (Spoiler alert - the added ingredient was nearly always cumin.)

Chilli con carne Recipe (Serves 4)

Ingredients

- 500g of minced beef
- 2 cloves of garlic
- 2 medium sized onions
- 2 red peppers (if available) or a handful of dried peppers
- 1 heaped heaped teaspoon of chilli powder
- 1 heaped teaspoon of cinnamon
- 2 x 400g tins of kidney beans
- 2 x 400g tins of tomatoes
- 1 beef stock cube (dissolved in 400g of boiling water)
- 2 tablespoons of vegetable oil to fry
- Salt and pepper to taste
- (1 tsp cumin – optional!)

Method: Peel and finely chop the onions and garlic. Halve the red peppers, remove the stalks and seeds and roughly chop. Heat 2 tablespoons of oil in a large casserole pan on a medium-high heat, add the chopped veg, chilli powder, and a pinch of sea salt and black pepper, then cook for 7 minutes, or until softened, stirring regularly. Drain and add the kidney beans, tip in the tomatoes, breaking them up with the back of a spoon, then pour in the stock. Add the minced beef, breaking any larger chunks. Bring to the boil, then reduce the heat to low and simmer with a lid slightly ajar for 1 hour, or until slightly thickened and reduced, stirring occasionally. Serve with rice or tortilla bread.

The origins of sticky toffee pudding are a sticky subject with many parts of the country and indeed the world claiming to have invented it. Owners of several hostelries including the Gait Inn in the East Riding of Yorkshire claim to have been serving it since 1907 (dubious). However, the Udny Arms Hotel in Aberdeenshire say that they invented it in the 1960s (also a bit iffy). Whatever its true provenance, the dessert reached a broader audience in the early 1970s, thanks largely to two chefs in Cumbria. Francis Coulson and Robert Lee served it at the Sharrow Bay Country House Hotel. The food critic Simon Hopkinson said that Coulson told him that he received the recipe from Lancastrian Patricia Martin who in turn got the recipe from Canadian air force officers who lodged at her hotel during the Second World War. Whatever its origins, it is a delicious, if filling, pudding. The phrase "leave room for pudding" is never more appropriate. It has since risen to be a staple of pub lunches, ready meals and is made at its best in the cafes and restaurants of Cumbria. Preferably when taking in a view of the lakes.

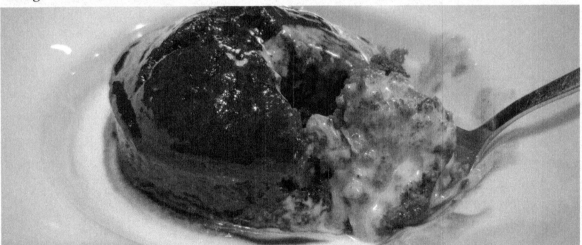

Sticky Toffee Pudding Recipe   (Serves 4)

Ingredients

For the sponge
- 200g dates
- 70g butter
- 200g demerara sugar
- 240g plain flour
- 3 eggs
- 1 tsp bicarbonate of soda
- 340g boiling water

For the toffee sauce
- 100g light brown sugar
- 50g butter
- 180g cream
- 1 tbsp treacle

Method: For the pudding mix, pour boiling water over dates and leave to soak for 30 mins to soften, then blitz in a food processor. Next, cream the butter and sugar together, then add the eggs and date mix. Finish by adding the flour and bicarbonate of soda, mix all together and make sure everything is fully combined. Pipe into greased moulds and cook in the oven at 160 degrees for 35 mins. For the toffee sauce, put all the ingredients in a pan and bring it to the boil. Pour the sauce over the sponge and serve with cream, ice cream or custard.

Fashion trends in 1974 saw bold designs and vivid colours focussing on browns, yellows, oranges and purples. Men's and women's hairstyles tended to be long. In this image the female model wears a floral pant suit whilst the male model sports a brightly striped shirt.

Bright solid block colours mixed with bold checks certainly make a statement in these matching outfits.

These four models are wearing brightly coloured South American inspired ponchos. The 1970s twist on the classic design is the ribbed roll-neck which became a key feature of the decade's fashion.

The maxi dress was another hugely popular design in 1974. This example is bursting with colour and floral patterns. Maxi dress designers included Jean Varon, Dereta, Katy, Biba and Julie.

One of the most recognisable features of 1970s fashion is the flared trouser which became known as bell-bottoms. This model is wearing flared jeans over brightly coloured platform shoes.

English actress Suzanna Leigh is pictured in a revealing bright yellow wrap dress accessorised with a blue bead necklace.

Pictured in Trafalgar Square, London amongst the infamous pigeons, this model is wearing a matching two-piece corduroy outfit with flared trousers. The brown ensemble is accessorised with a mustard yellow handbag.

Photographed in London, playwright and author Alan Bennett is sporting a classic wide necktie with a bold spotted design. Vivid shirts and ties were a fashion trend for men.

The Rise of the Package Holiday

By the early 1970s Britons took nearly six million trips abroad for a holiday, far fewer that the 47 million trips of today. Around half of the excursions were by ferry, with flying still being seen as an expensive treat. Coach trips via ferry were common, with some going as far as northern Italy but also to Holland and Belgium. Germany was very popular, particularly Bavaria. When Britons did travel by air, they were sure to make the most of their trip. If the flight cost was 60 percent of the total holiday price, people would want to go away for a couple of weeks. Packages would usually be for 14 nights. 1969 brought the

Coach trips to Europe were very popular in 1974

unveiling of the Boeing 747, which allowed airlines to pack passengers in more closely. This helped to democratise flying. The aircraft entered service in January 1970 with a Pan Am flight from New York to London. Aircraft crashes were more common in the seventies. 1972 was the most dangerous year in civilian aviation history; 2,432 people died in 56 accidents involving passenger flights. In contrast, 2019 was the third safest with 267 people dying in 14 accidents. It was not uncommon for passengers to say a prayer at the beginning of a flight and

Soaking up the sun on a package holiday

applaud the pilot on landing. Familiarity was a serious selling point. Package tour providers often advertised their trips with the promise of a home-from-home experience. The UK, but with better weather. The cover of a 1970s Thomson Sky Tours brochure features two women smiling in front of clear, blue sky and a young family playing in a swimming pool. There's nothing in the pictures to determine the subjects' location. A trio of Lunn Poly and Panorama brochures from the same year also focused on the pool and exotic-looking cocktails. Holidaymakers would often return with tales of bumping into people from their local neighbourhood proclaiming it to be a "small world". This was far from a coincidence as they more than likely saw the same advert in the local travel agent's window. The suntan was back in fashion. Previously having a tan meant that you worked outdoors, now it was a sign that you could afford a holiday in the sun lying on the beach in one of the Costas. All this was having a detrimental effect on the traditional British holiday, particularly the seaside resorts which saw a slow and steady decline. Large hotels that had once been full, now lay half empty and some were forced to close. One growth area in the domestic holiday market was youth hostelling. In fact growth was so rapid that the Youth Hostel Association was in desperate need of more accommodation to meet demand. An example solution was found at Ambleside in the Lake District, where the run down Queen's Hotel was converted into a 134-bed hostel. Residents could now enjoy magnificent views of Lake Windermere at a fraction of the cost of staying in the former hotel.

Ambleside on the banks of Lake Windermere

Christmas 1974

Christmas is great, but it's hard not to look back and wonder if it was even better in the days before iPads, smartphones and festive adverts that begin in October. Here are a few reasons why Christmas in the 1970s was so magical. First the decorations. Forget every spare square inch being covered in Christmas lights before the end of November, in most homes in the 1970s the tree and decorations only went up about a week before the big day. All the tinsel, coloured lights, foil hanging decorations and crepe paper streamers would be carefully brought out of storage from the year before, with new paper chains being prepared as required. Baubles were big news; the more brightly coloured the better. The countdown to the big day was marked on the traditional Advent calendar, but it was more than likely to have only a small pictorial scene behind the paper door such as a robin in the snow, rather than the chocolates or other treats you see today. With only three channels to choose from and no videos or DVDs in sight, the chances were that you and the rest of the

Helping mum decorate the tree

country were watching pretty much the same thing at the same time in the Seventies. The Basil Brush Show, Bruce Forsyth's Generation Game, Billy Smart's Christmas Circus, To The Manor Born, the annual star-studded BBC panto and The Good Old Days were all among the festive favourites. But there were two stand-outs that truly brought the nation together. Christmas dinners up and down the country were planned around the Queen's Speech at 3pm, while the Morecambe and Wise Christmas specials kept the whole family entertained

Rolling a giant snowball in the park

with big names such as newsreader Angela Rippon and conductor André Previn playing along for laughs. With the exception of 1974, the duo were Christmas Day fixtures and their 1977 special scored one of the highest ever audiences in British television history with more than 20 million viewers. Children might have started the day with Puffa Puffa Rice or Pink Panther Flakes for breakfast, but before long they were ripping into their Selection Box. Adults might have a full English breakfast, before quaffing a snowball (advocaat and lemonade). There was still enough room for turkey and all the trimmings though, washed down with a glass of Blue Nun or Black Tower wine; for the adults at least. After dinner, mince pies and pudding would often be accompanied by a cheeky splash of port or sherry. To really get things in full swing, a Party Seven (a tin can containing seven pints of ale) might be wheeled out, just as long as dad was able to open it. A screwdriver and hammer were usually required, then it was like Mount Vesuvius. The festivities would continue into Boxing Day, with more chocolates and more drinking. Relatives and neighbours might be invited over with cold meats and canapés being the order of the day.

A classic Snowball at Xmas

Cinema attendance in the UK, which had hit a record low in 1973, recovered to 138 million visits in 1974, an increase of 4 million. This was due in no small part to the films that were on offer. 1974 was a classic year for cinema, with some truly outstanding movies coming to our screens. *The Godfather Part II*, *Chinatown* and *The Taking of Pelham One Two Three*, to name but a few. There were also some big blockbusters. *Towering Inferno* boasted an all-star cast and became the biggest grossing film to date. Another disaster movie that drew the crowds in was *Earthquake*, starring Charlton Heston and Ava Gardner. It was the first film to use Sensurround, a series of large speakers aimed at replicating a real earthquake. But, in reality, it sounded more like the cinema was too close to a busy railway station. The year saw the ninth incarnation of James Bond, but to mixed reviews. There was also a remake of Noel Coward's

Francis Ford Coppola directed The Godfather Part II

1945 classic *Brief Encounter*. Instead of the rather stiff upper lipped Trevor Howard and Celia Johnson, the producers cast Richard Burton and Sophia Loren. It didn't work. Burton's public persona meant that it was hard to believe that the five times married star wouldn't have tried to book them in to the nearest hotel under the names of Mr. and Mrs. Smith upon their first encounter. It was also a classic year for horror, with *The Exorcist* winning at the Oscars and *The Texas Chainsaw Massacre* shocking audiences, in spite of containing very little on-screen violence. It was a great year for fans of all music genres. Bob Dylan released his

Jason Miller and Max von Sydow in The Exorcist

fourteenth studio album *Planet Waves*, which featured the anthemic *Forever Young*, not once but twice. The rock band Yes sold out Madison Square Gardens two nights running without even advertising, giving us a taste of the power of stadium rock that was to come. Helen Reddy had her third US number one with the frankly quite weird *Angie Baby* and was rewarded with an American Music Award. In soul music, Stevie Wonder won a Grammy for best album with *Innervisions* and Roberta Flack's *Killing Me Softly With His Song* won best single. In Brighton, Agnetha, Benny, Björn and Anni-Frid, aka ABBA, won the Eurovision Song Contest with their song *Waterloo*, which kick-started their career as one of the greatest pop bands of all time. British television saw the debuts of two of the most enduring sitcoms of all time, namely *Rising Damp* and *Porridge*. Both starred Richard Beckinsale. In the first he played a hippy student, in the latter a prisoner. This necessitated him wearing a rather unconvincing wig in *Rising Damp*. US television featured large on the British small screen and we all became accustomed to the phrases "Goodnight John Boy" and "Who loves ya baby?", when *The Waltons* and *Kojak* made their UK debuts.

ABBA won the Eurovision Song Contest in Brighton in 1974

The Godfather Part II

Directed by Francis Ford Coppola
Starring Al Pacino, Diane Keaton and Robert De Niro
Released 12th December 1974

Al Pacino

This sequel (and also a prequel) to *The Godfather* is split between the stories of Michael Corleone (Al Pacino) and a young Vito Corleone (Robert De Niro in his first Oscar-winning performance). In the 1950s, Michael is trying to expand his crime empire to places such as Las Vegas, Hollywood and even Cuba. However, there are numerous problems as older brother Fredo (John Cazale) may have double-crossed the family. Also two prominent crime bosses pose a considerable threat. Younger sister Connie (Talia Shire) is still reeling from her husband's murder and her father's death at the conclusion of the original film. Michael is also distancing himself from his wife (Diane Keaton) and some of his most trusted friends. While all this is occurring, we get glimpses into the early life of Michael's father. We learn that his parents and older brother have been killed in early-1900s Sicily and that he has migrated to New York. Vito pays his dues and learns the tricks of the trade, biding his time, before deciding to create his own small empire which would of course grow and become what we saw in the original. It would seem that the film would be confusing by jumping back and forth between Michael and his father, but that is not so. Coppola gives you just enough information to keep the audience intrigued through each segment.

The Taking of Pelham One Two Three

Directed by John Sargent
Starring Walter Matthau and Robert Shaw
Released on 17th September 1964

Walter Matthau

Four men board train Pelham 123, on the New York subway, at successive stations. They are each dressed similarly and each wears glasses and has a moustache; they also use obviously false names; Mr. Blue, Mr. Green, Mr. Brown and Mr. Grey. Shortly after boarding they take control of the train and force the driver to stop. They then split the train and continue further down the line in the front carriage. The authorities quickly realise something is wrong but it isn't until the hijackers respond to their call that they know just what has happened. The hijackers want one million dollars within the hour and threaten to shoot one hostage per minute after the hour is up. The person responsible for defusing the situation is NYC Transit Authority police lieutenant Garber (Matthau). He must try to figure out how the hijackers hope to escape and tries to buy more time to raise the ransom. This is a taut thriller with almost no extraneous material wasting no time establishing characters. We do learn a little about them: Mr. Blue is a British mercenary who saw action in Africa and Green was a former subway driver. We also learn that one of the hostages is an off duty cop but have no idea which one. Once the hijacking is underway the tension is quickly raised and things stay tense till the end. The film was remade in 2009 starring Denzel Washington and John Travolta.

American Graffiti

Directed by George Lucas
Starring Richard Dreyfuss, Candy Clarke and Harrison Ford
UK Release: 28th March 1974

It's the summer of 1962 in a small town in California. One evening, we spend time following various teenagers on the brink of adulthood. There's a college-bound young guy with doubts about leaving, there's a nerd who gets a date with a blonde fox, there's a drag racer who gets lumbered with a thirteen-year-old girl and all the while a DJ called Wolfman Jack plays music throughout the night on the local radio. There are street gangs with logo'd leather jackets, waitresses on roller-skates and continual car cruising. There's no real plot, it's all about a moment in time. When it was released in 1973, it told of a time a decade in the past but it truly seemed like an aeon away on account of the transition of the counter-cultural 60's when everything changed so dramatically and radically. The early 60's pre-Vietnam small town America seemed like an alien landscape, one with more innocence and clearly one that held much appeal in the cynical landscape of 70's America. Due to the low budget, George Lucas was unable to pay all of the crew members. He offered to give many of them a screen credit in lieu of payment, and they accepted. Traditionally, only department heads received screen a credit. Giving screen credits to so many crew members has now become a tradition, which is why closing credits last so long now.

Murder on the Orient Express

Directed by Sidney Lumet
Starring Albert Finney, Sean Connery, Ingrid Bergman, John Gielgud
Released: 21st November 1974

Ingrid Bergman won an Oscar for her performance

Albert Finney's only outing as Agatha Christie's Belgian sleuth Hercule Poirot gained the rare approval of the author, who declared Sidney Lumet's film of her 1934 mystery novel to be one of the very few adaptations of her work that she really enjoyed. Christie did however express disappointment with the small size of Finney's moustache in the film, undoubtedly inspiring Kenneth Branagh to take the 'tache spectacle' to the next level when he took up the Poirot mantle in 2017. Lumet's film, scripted by Paul Dehn and Anthony Shaffer (uncredited), is by far the superior adaptation, providing an exercise in dynamic visual storytelling from its opening sequence depicting a 'Lindbergh-esque' kidnapping onwards. It also makes fantastic use of its outstanding ensemble cast, among them Lauren Bacall, Ingrid Bergman, Sean Connery, John Gielgud, Vanessa Redgrave and Anthony Perkins. Of course, as you would expect from a Poirot adaptation every "Madame, Mademoiselle and Monsieur" is a suspect, but once Poirot has supped his tisane, his 'little grey cells' begin to work and the murderer/murderers are revealed. As compelling as the mystery plot is, the film works best as an A-list actors' showcase and kicked off a run of starry Christie adaptations. Of all the star-studded cast, Ingrid Bergman stood out. She won the Academy Award for Best Supporting Actress.

Paul Newman

The Towering Inferno

Directed by John Guillermin
Starring Steve McQueen, Paul Newman, Faye Dunaway and William Holden
Released: 16th December 1974

The story unfolds in a state-of-the-art, 138-story skyscraper in San Francisco, during its grand opening celebration. However, a small fire starts due to electrical issues, rapidly escalating into an inferno, trapping hundreds of people on the upper floors. As the fire rages out of control, the building's architect, Doug Roberts (Newman) and the fire chief, Michael O'Hallorhan (McQueen), must collaborate to rescue as many people as possible. The film portrays the intense efforts of firefighters and civilians as they battle the blaze and struggle to survive. The film is renowned for its spectacular special effects and realistic portrayal of a high-rise fire disaster. It received critical acclaim for its thrilling suspense, powerful performances and groundbreaking visual effects, winning three Academy Awards. It explores themes like corporate negligence, heroism and the human spirit in the face of catastrophe. The film features a stellar cast including Fred Astaire and Robert Vaughan. Even O.J. Simpson makes an appearance. The big issue was how could the producers keep all of these big egos happy? William Holden demanded top billing. However his career was in decline and his last major role was in 1969's *The Wild Bunch*. He was eventually placated and was billed after Steve McQueen and Paul Newman in exchange for a higher cut of the box office. As a result he ended up earning more than the two top-billings.

Roger Moore

The Man With the Golden Gun

Directed by Guy Hamilton   Theme sung by Lulu
Starring Roger Moore, Christopher Lee and Britt Ekland
Released: 18th December 1974

In this, the ninth Bond film and the second to star Roger Moore, the killer Scaramanga (Christopher Lee) uses a special golden gun for his assignments and has a rare birthmark on his chest. These are about the only things the movie has in common with the novel which is set in the Caribbean, whereas the movie takes us to Thailand, where Scaramanga secretly works with solar energy. Casting Herve Villechaize was an attempt to create a sidekick for Scaramanga like Oddjob had been to Goldfinger, a bit too silly in the end. Being a child of its time, the film couldn't resist some half-hearted kung fu. Somehow parts of the movie seem artificial, especially the mirror labyrinth where Scaramanga likes to practice the art of killing. But the beautiful islands will stick in the memory and the film includes some amazing car chases. There is an interesting promo photo for the movie with Lee and Moore back to back, gun in hand. This is not just a duel, this is also illustrating the idea of Scaramanga being a 'dark Bond', his mirror image as a bad guy with the same skills, but different ideology. "We have so much in common, Mr Bond", Scaramanga says. "Ours is the loneliest profession." Derek Malcolm of the Guardian hated the film saying "the script is the limpest of the lot and... Roger Moore as 007 is the last man on earth to make it sound better than it is."

The Conversation

Gene Hackman

Directed by Francis Ford Coppola
Starring Gene Hackman and John Cazale
Released: 7th April 1974

When one thinks of Francis Ford Coppola, three of his masterpieces typically spring to mind: *The Godfather*, *The Godfather: Part II* and *Apocalypse Now*. Less mentioned, but more relevant to our privacy-challenged world, is 1974's *The Conversation*. The film earned Coppola two Oscar nominations: Best Screenplay and Best Picture. He ended up losing to himself, winning both prizes for *The Godfather: Part II* instead! Gene Hackman stars as Harry Caul, a surveillance expert. The film's title refers to Harry's most recent job. With the help of a team of spies, Harry records a conversation between a young man and woman strolling around San Francisco's crowded Union Square. The woman is the wife of a powerful businessman who hires Harry, ostensibly to provide evidence of her infidelity. He also gives strict orders for Harry to deliver the recorded conversation to him personally. So when the businessman's underling, played by Harrison Ford, aggressively tries to intercept it, red flags are raised. Harry keeps the tape analyses it for clues. Within the distorted gibberish he detects the pronouncement: "He'd kill us if he had the chance." Fearing he's stumbled across a possible murder plot, Harry becomes increasingly paranoid. *The Conversation* is a classic thriller, but it's Coppola's nuanced exploration of Harry's life that lifts it out of the ordinary.

Swallows and Amazons

Directed by Claude Whatham
Starring Virginia McKenna and Simon West
Released: 13th June 1974

Four young children, John (Simon West), Susan (Suzanna Hamilton), Titty (Sophie Neville) and Roger (Stephen Grendon), arrive in the Lake District with their mother (Virginia McKenna) for a summer break. Their father, a sea captain, is away on a voyage on the other side of the world. Their holiday home is right beside a long lake and the children immediately find their attention drawn to a large uninhabited island in the middle. They are allowed to use a small wooden sailing boat named 'The Swallow' to explore the lake and the island. Before long they come up with the idea of setting up a camp on the island. Two girls, Peggy (Lesley Bennett) and Nancy (Kit Seymour), a.k.a 'The Amazons', arrive on the scene and challenge the Swallows to a test of courage and cunning to decide the true rulers of the lake. The film manages to capture the spirit of adventure and exploration rather nicely and is a treat to look at throughout. Individual scenes work quite well, such as the bit with the charcoal burners and the night-time sortie in which the Swallows attempt to steal the Amazons' boat. The film was made in the summer of 1973 and is as much a travelogue as a story. Suzanne Hamilton revealed in an interview in 2023 that the film was made on four different lakes: Coniston Water, Windermere, Elterwater, Derwentwater and a smelly lily pond.

The Exorcist | Best Screenplay and 1 other

Starring Ellen Burstyn, Max von Sydow and Linda Blair
Directed by William Friedkin
Released: 26th December 1973 (USA)

Publicity still with Linda Blair and Ellen Burstyn

The Exorcist has become the horror movie by which other horror movies are judged. It has been imitated many times, but never equalled. The story concerns a mother (Ellen Burstyn) and her possessed daughter Regan (Linda Blair). Two priests, Karras (Jason Miller) and Merrin (Max Von Sydow), attempt to free Regan from possession by the devil. Meanwhile, a Police Inspector (Lee J. Cobb) is investigating ever stranger events. The priests take incredible risks trying to unravel the mystery of the demons living inside Regan. This is a suspenseful and horrifying story. The movie starts strong and grows more and more tense up to the scary and eerie finale. This is a first-rate film, thanks to fine acting, tight pacing and skillful special effects with magnificent make-up by Dick Smith. On the first day of filming the exorcism sequence, Linda Blair's delivery of her foul-mouthed dialogue so disturbed the gentlemanly Max Von Sydow that he actually forgot his lines. The script is bold, the acting excellent and the direction by William Friedkin has plenty of good pace and conviction. It has dark cinematography by Owen Roitzman creating a sinister and mysterious atmosphere. The foreboding soundtrack comes from Mike Oldfield's *Tubular Bells*. Due to death threats against Linda Blair from religious zealots who believed the film "glorified Satan", the makers Warner Brothers had bodyguards protecting her for six months after the film's release.

The Sting | Best Picture and 6 others

Starring Paul Newman, Robert Redford and Robert Shaw
Directed by George Roy Hill
Released: 25th December 1973 (USA)

Henry Gondorff (Newman) and Johnny Hooker (Redford) are two con artists seeking revenge against a powerful and dangerous mobster named Doyle Lonnegan, played by Robert Shaw. The story revolves around a meticulously planned 'sting' (con) that Gondorff and Hooker orchestrate to take down Lonnegan. They create an elaborate scheme involving a fake off-track betting parlour and a fictitious bookie named Shaw, designed to make Lonnegan believe he's being outsmarted by a rival gangster. As the plot unfolds, the audience is taken through a series of twists, turns and double-crosses, keeping them on the edge of their seats. The movie is renowned for its clever dialogue, intricate plotting and period charm. It captures the essence of the 1930s with its art deco visual style, jazz-infused soundtrack and attention to detail in the costumes and set designs. The performances by Newman and Redford are top-notch, showcasing their on-screen chemistry and natural charisma. Beyond its entertainment value, the film explores themes of loyalty, trust and the art of deception. It delves into the world of confidence games where nothing is as it seems, and everyone has their own agenda. The climax features a thrilling twist that leaves the audience in awe of the characters' ingenuity and audacity. It was a critical and commercial success, receiving seven Academy Awards, including Best Picture, Best Director and Best Original Screenplay.

Kojak

Starring Telly Savalas, George Savalas and Dan Frazer
First aired in UK: 24th August 1974 on BBC1

Telly Savalas as Kojak

Created and written by Abby Mann, who won an Oscar for the film *Judgement at Nuremberg* (1961), *Kojak* is an American crime drama television series that aired from 1973 to 1978. The series starred Telly Savalas as the bald, tough and no-nonsense detective Lieutenant Theo Kojak, who works for the New York City Police Department. Kojak's catchphrase "Who loves ya, baby?" entered the popular lexicon of the 1970s. The show's premise revolves around *Kojak* solving crimes in the gritty streets of New York City, while dealing with the bureaucracy and corruption within the police department. He is often seen sucking on his trademark lollipop, which he uses to calm his nerves during intense situations. In reality, Telly Savalas used it in order to try to give up smoking. The series was notable for its realistic portrayal of police work and its focus on social issues such as racism, drug abuse and corruption. It also featured Detective Stavros, played by George Savalas, Telly's real-life brother. *Kojak* was a critical and commercial success, earning four Emmy nominations and a Golden Globe Award for Telly Savalas. The show's popularity led to several made-for-television movies and a short-lived revival in the late 1980s. Today, *Kojak* remains a beloved and influential television series, remembered for its iconic characters and gripping storytelling. In all, the series ran for 117 episodes. In 2005, the series was rebooted for a short-lived single season with African-American actor Ving Rhames taking the lead role.

Porridge

First aired: 5th September 1974
Starring Ronnie Barker, Richard Beckinsale and Fulton McKay

Ronnie Barker

The first episode of Ronnie Barker's much loved sitcom *Porridge* was broadcast on 5th September 1974. Barker starred as Norman Stanley Fletcher, an habitual criminal who accepts arrest as an occupational hazard, serving time in HMP Slade. It was written by Dick Clements and Ian La Frenais, who managed to mine comedy gold from the disparate characters banged up together, while not ignoring the unpleasant facts of prison life. Fletcher shared a cell with the impressionable Godber, played by Richard Beckinsale. Other prisoners were played by a fine cast, including Brian Glover, Christopher Biggins, Tony Osoba, David Jason and Peter Vaughan. Fulton McKay played the strict prison officer Mr. McKay, while Brian Wilde was the gentler and more gullible Mr. Barrowclough, showing two extremes of authority. The only regular female role was Fletcher's daughter Ingrid, played by Patricia Brake. The characters of Fletcher, Mr. McKay and Mr. Barrington were first seen in the pilot, *Prisoner and Escort*, which aired as part of Barker's *Seven of One* series the previous year. *Porridge* ran for three series until 1977, with two Christmas specials. In the final episode, Godber is released on parole and goes on holiday with Ingrid. Brake and Beckinsale were back with Barker in *Going Straight*, which followed Fletcher's life after his release. There was also a *Porridge* feature film. *Porridge* is frequently voted among the top sitcoms of all time.

Mr. Men

First aired: 31st December 1974

Narrated by Arthur Lowe

The animated Mr. Men series was based on the books by Roger Hargreaves. In 1971, Hargreaves' eldest son Adam asked him a peculiar question: "What does a tickle look like?" In response, Hargreaves penned the tale of the long-armed, lovable rogue *Mr. Tickle*. Once published, Mr. Tickle became a runaway success, selling one million copies within the first three years. Over the next couple of years, Hargreaves would create 12 more of his iconic characters. The BBC produced an animated series, *The Mr. Men Show*, voiced and narrated by Arthur Lowe of Dad's Army. It was first shown on 31st December 1974 with *Mr. Happy* starring. By 1975 the single story format had given way to a double-bill in which two Mr. Men stories were told back to back with Arthur Lowe asking us "which Mr. Man we might care to meet next?", then humming the Mr. Men tune between the two stories. This was followed by a second series a year later. Over the coming years, the Mr. Men gang would venture into a range of other mediums, Starting in 1977, British newspapers The Mirror and Daily Mail published a Mr. Men comic strip, and in 1979 BBC records released *The Mr. Men Songs*. By the end of the 70s, Hargreaves had created 39 Mr. Men characters, and it was time for something new. The first Little Miss character, *Little Miss Bossy*, was brought to life in 1981 followed swiftly by several others. A *Little Miss* animated series was produced in 1983.

Rising Damp

First broadcast: 2nd September 1974

Starring: Leonard Rossiter, Frances de la Tour, Don Warrington and Richard Beckinsale

It will come as no surprise that *Rising Damp* began its life as a stage play. The TV series was filmed in front of a live audience in a nod to its origins. In the series we meet Rigsby (Rossiter), a live-in slum landlord and war veteran with unreconstructed views on modern society. Into the mix come the tenants. Alan Moore (Beckinsale) is a medical student with little get-up-and-go and too much hair for Rigsby's liking. Philip Smith (Warrington) was born in Croydon, but claims to be descended from West African nobility and is suave and educated. He lies about his 'primitive' background, clearly mocking the views held by Rigsby. Then there is the chaste and chased Miss Jones (de la Tour) who is the object of Rigsby's cravings. Another significant recurring character is Vienna the cat, who gets mistreated by the landlord when things don't go according to plan. The series never misses a beat and unlike most 1970s comedy, is watchable today. In the *Charisma* episode of 1974, Rigsby's gullibility and desperation lead him to believe in Philip's 'Love Wood', a piece of fictitious 'African folk law'. When the wood fails to lure Miss Jones, Rigby is left crestfallen and kicks the cat. Explaining the racial sub-plot, Warrington told *The Telegraph* in 2013: "The difficulty for Rigsby lies in observing somebody who is exactly who he would like to be apart from the fact that he is black, and that's very confusing for him."

The Waltons

First aired in the UK: 18th Feb 1974 on BBC2

Starring Mary Elizabeth McDonough, Richard Thomas and Ralph Waite

John, John-Boy and Olivia

The Waltons was an American television series that aired in the US from 1972 to 1981 and created by Earl Hamner Jr. It depicted the lives of the Walton family during the Great Depression and World War II in the rural community of Walton's Mountain in Virginia. The series revolves around John Walton Sr., his wife Olivia and their seven children: John Boy, Jason, Mary Ellen, Erin, Ben, Jim Bob, and Elizabeth. The family faces various challenges such as financial struggles, personal conflicts and the impact of historical events on their lives. Despite these hardships, they find strength in their love for each other and their strong sense of community. John Boy, the eldest son and a budding writer, serves as the show's narrator, often reflecting on the lessons learned from the family's experiences. The relationships between the siblings, their parents, and their neighbours form the heart of the show, showcasing themes of family values, resilience, and the importance of community support. In the signature scene that closes almost every episode, the family house is enveloped in darkness, save for a few lights in the upstairs bedrooms. Then two or more characters make some brief references to that episode's events, then bid each other goodnight, after which the lights go out. The show received critical acclaim for its portrayal of American family life and its nostalgic depiction of a simpler time. It won numerous awards during its run, including multiple Emmy Awards and Golden Globes.

Tom's Midnight Garden

Aired January 7th to Jan 21st 1974 (in three parts)

Based on a book by Philippa Pearce

Illustrative image

Forced to stay with his childless aunt and uncle for the summer holidays while his brother convalesces from measles, Tom Lang is lonely and bored. The only fascination he has is with an old grandfather clock that stands in the hallway. The only thing Tom knows about it is that he must never touch it. Lying in bed unable to sleep one night, he hears the clock strike 13. Creeping downstairs to investigate whilst the rest of the house sleeps he throws open the back garden door and crosses the threshold into a magical Victorian garden of the 1880s. Nervously at first, Tom explores. Of the four children that live in the house with the magnificent summer garden only one, an unhappy orphan called Hatty, seems able to see him, and she thinks he is a ghost. Quite a reasonable assumption as Tom doesn't appear to leave footprints or cast a shadow and is able to walk through walls and doors. But the pair soon begin to strike up a wonderful friendship playing absorbing games, climbing trees and hiding in special places. Each night, Tom and Hatty explore the garden and its mysteries. They form an intense bond which brings them close together but which, ultimately, breaks them apart. With each subsequent visit Hatty seems to be growing up fast, and as she grows up the bond between them wanes. The book on which the series is based is regarded as a classic. The last meeting between the youthful Tom and the elderly Hatty is one of the most poignant scenes in children's literature.

The Birth of Commercial Radio

Before 1973, with the exception of off-shore 'pirate' stations, radio listeners in Britain had to content themselves with four main BBC stations alongside some local radio, also run by the BBC. In 1973, two challengers to the BBC monopoly emerged in the form of LBC and Capital Radio, both broadcasting to London. 1974 saw an expansion of commercial radio and other major conurbations in the UK saw independent radio licences being granted. The most significant one was in Manchester. At 5am on Tuesday 2nd April 1974, Piccadilly Radio 261 began jangling out of transistors across Greater Manchester. A newsreader told listeners that the foreign secretary, James Callaghan, was about to get tough with the EEC. The bright-as-a-button new Piccadilly DJ Roger Day, formerly of pirate stations Radios Caroline and Luxembourg, played *Good Vibrations* by his beloved Beach Boys and then a flurry of compressed close-harmony jingles. Piccadilly Radio brought new levels of localism and bounce to Manchester. Colin Walters, the programme controller, placed great store in local news, phone-ins, outside broadcasts and football as well as promoting the station with t-shirts and car-stickers. The newsroom was well-staffed and well-qualified, and the sports desk defiantly partisan. Reporters Tom Tyrell and Brian Clarke were die-hard United and City fans respectively and they didn't hide their biases. The advertising sales team was especially energetic, and radio ads and promos for local firm. Washway Car Wash, crashed up against noisy slots for Lookers Ford Dealership. Piccadilly was catnip to schoolkids, college students, shop floor workers, taxi and bus drivers alike. There was also a popular weekly show called *Tripe & Onions* aimed at young children.

Roger Day in 2016

Cold Comfort Farm

Written by Stella Gibbons and first published in 1932
Ran for 6 episodes from the 9th December 1974 on BBC Radio 4

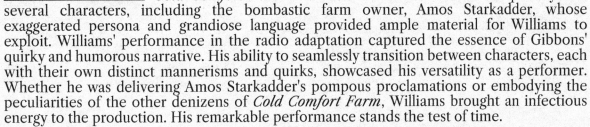
Kenneth Williams

In 1974, Kenneth Williams brought his inimitable talent to the radio adaptation of Stella Gibbons' classic comedic novel *Cold Comfort Farm*. Williams, renowned for his wit and timing, perfectly embodied the eccentric characters populating Gibbons' fictional farmstead. Set in rural England, the book follows the story of Flora Poste, a young woman who, after the death of her parents, finds herself in need of a place to live. She decides to impose herself upon her distant relatives, the Starkadders, who reside in the dilapidated *Cold Comfort Farm*. Williams lends his voice to the portrayal of several characters, including the bombastic farm owner, Amos Starkadder, whose exaggerated persona and grandiose language provided ample material for Williams to exploit. Williams' performance in the radio adaptation captured the essence of Gibbons' quirky and humorous narrative. His ability to seamlessly transition between characters, each with their own distinct mannerisms and quirks, showcased his versatility as a performer. Whether he was delivering Amos Starkadder's pompous proclamations or embodying the peculiarities of the other denizens of *Cold Comfort Farm*, Williams brought an infectious energy to the production. His remarkable performance stands the test of time.

Elton John

Don't Let the Sun Go Down on Me
Music by Elton John   Words by Bernie Taupin
Released: 20th May 1974

This is a song that was influenced by The Beach Boys, and contains contributions from members of the group; Carl Wilson and Bruce Johnston both sang backing vocals. Elton said the Beach Boys' sound, harmonies and the way they structured their songs was an influence on many of his tracks. Regarding the composition of this song, lyricist Bernie Taupin said: "My only recollections of this is that we wanted to write something big. I mean, big in that dramatic Spectory (as in Phil Spector) style, like *You've Lost That Loving Feelin'.* Hopefully being powerful without being pompous. I'm not sure that with this in mind it made me fashion the lyrics any differently." Elton claims he would not have attempted a song like this early in his career. He felt his voice had improved over the years and by 1974, he had enough confidence and ability to sing with a very broad range.

John Denver

Annie's Song (You Fill Up My Senses)
Written and recorded by John Denver
Released: June 1974

Denver wrote this for his then-wife Ann Martell after their first separation and near break up of their marriage in 1974. He said that it was one of the fastest songs he ever wrote, composing it in about 10 minutes while riding a ski lift in Aspen, Colorado. Denver was reflecting on all the joy he found in his marriage and his relief that they were back together. Denver recalled: "Suddenly, I'm hypersensitive to how beautiful everything is. All of these things filled up my senses, and when I said this to myself, unbidden images came one after the other. All of the pictures merged and I was left with Annie. That song was the embodiment of the love I felt at that time." Annie said the day Denver wrote the song: "It was written after John and I had gone through a pretty intense time together. Initially it was a love song and it was given to me through him, and yet for him it became a bit like a prayer."

Leonard Cohen

Chelsea Hotel #2
Written and recorded by Leonard Cohen
Released: 30th August 1974

The Chelsea Hotel in New York city is where Cohen lived when he wasn't at his home in Montreal or his cottage on the Greek Island of Hydra. He chose the Chelsea because he heard he would meet people with a similar artistic bent, which he did. When introducing this song in concert, he would often tell a story about meeting a famous singer in an elevator of the Chelsea, which led to the sexual encounter he describes in this song. Leonard Cohen sometimes admitted that he wrote it about a very brief affair he had with Janis Joplin in 1968, explaining that she came to the *Chelsea Hotel* looking for Kris Kristofferson, and when she and Cohen ended up in an elevator together, he told her he was Kristofferson. She knew he wasn't, but figured he would do on this particular evening. "We fell into each others arms through some process of elimination", Cohen said.

The McCartneys

Live and Let Die

Written by Paul and Linda McCartney
Winner of the Academy Award for Best Original Song: 2nd April 1974

When the producers of the eighth James Bond movie, *Live and Let Die*, approached Paul McCartney to write the theme song, the ever meticulous former Beatle requested a copy of the book. After reading it in one day, he and his wife Linda produced what many believe to be the greatest 'Bond' song of all time. It starts off with piano and McCartney's doubled-up vocals and slowly builds up to a sudden, fiery explosion of instruments which are something people have grown accustomed to when watching any James Bond film. It is like a gift box filled with surprises. The styles incorporated into this song would have been a hit-or-miss for anyone else, but of course, not for Paul McCartney. He's one of the few who can transform songs from the mediocre to the magical. It reached No.1 in the US cash box chart but only reached No.9 in the UK.

Barbra Streisand

The Way We Were

Performed by Barbra Streisand
US Billboard #1 on 2nd February 1974

This was the title track to the movie of the same name, which starred Streisand and Robert Redford. The song is about a couple who fall deeply in love despite being complete opposites. They are looking back on fond memories of their time together. This song is famous for its opening line, "Memories, light the corners of my mind", which sets the nostalgic tone for the song and makes it perfect for the movie. Early demos of the song reveal that the first word was written as "Daydreams". Streisand came up with the idea to change it to "Memories", although needing it shortened to two syllables to fit the music, it becomes "Mem'ries". Streisand also released an album called *The Way We Were* featuring the song, but was sued by the movie's producer. Streisand's album was re-issued as *Barbra Streisand Featuring The Way We Were and All In Love Is Fair*. Despite the clumsy title, the album went to #1 and outsold the soundtrack.

David Essex

Rock On

Written and performed by David Essex
UK Charts #3 US Cash Box Charts #1 in March 1974

David Essex wrote this to play at the end of the 1973 movie *That'll Be The Day*, where he played a working-class, aspiring rocker in pre-Beatles England. Essex spent much of the '60s making unsuccessful recordings, but did far better as an actor, landing the role of Jesus in the London production of *Godspell* in 1971. This earned him the role of Jim MacLaine in *That'll Be The Day*, starring with Ringo Starr and Keith Moon. Essex asked the film's producer David Puttnam if he could write the ending song. During the eight weeks of filming, Essex came up with *Rock On*, a song that embodies the restless and rebellious nature of his character amid the backdrop of rock and roll. Puttnam thought it was "too weird", so it didn't make the film. However, Essex used it to get a record deal with CBS, which released it as his first single on the label. The song was an international hit.

ABBA

Waterloo

Written and Performed by ABBA   Released: 4th March 1974

Waterloo is the place where Napoleon Bonaparte met his defeat at an epic battle in 1815. This song uses the battle as a metaphor for a woman who gives in and falls in love with a man: he's her 'Waterloo'. Originally recorded in Swedish, it was ABBA's English language version that won the Eurovision Song Contest in Brighton in 1974, propelling the band on to the world stage. Even though the song constantly repeats the name of the battle that spelt the end of Napoleon's empire, the French, like the rest of Europe, were more than happy to buy this song in large quantities. The single spent 12 weeks in the French charts, peaking at #3. In Belgium, where the Battle of Waterloo took place, the song spent five weeks at #1. Curiously at the contest, the British jury gave the Swedish quartet 'nul points' for what was clearly the best Eurovision song ever. It seems that they saw it as the main threat to their entry, Olivia Newton John's *Long Live Love*.

Barry White

You're My First, You're My Last, My Everything

Performed by Barry White   Released: 29th October 1974

White's friend Peter Sterling Radcliffe started writing this as a country song called *You're My First, You're My Last, My In-Between*, but he couldn't get it recorded for 21 years. When White was down on his luck, Radcliffe bought his children toys for Christmas; a kindness White didn't forget when he became famous. So when Radcliffe offered him the song, he didn't hesitate to hear it. Tony Sepe, another songwriter who was in the room, laughed when he heard the country song with the clip-clop of horses' hooves keeping the rhythm. He was shocked by White's positive reaction. Changing the genre from country to disco, White kept the chord changes and part of Radcliffe's melody but also added his own melody and nearly all new lyrics. "I heard what was inside that song", White explained. "Half of the words in it I changed right in front of the microphone." When Radcliffe heard the final result, he cried. This was White's third #1 single on the R&B chart.

Charles Aznavour

She

Performed by Charles Aznavour   Written by Aznavour and Kretzmer

UK #1 from 29th June to 20th July 1974

This was the theme from the UK TV series *The Seven Faces of Women*. It was written by Herbert Kretzmer, the lyricist of *Les Miserables*, and Aznavour, who wrote the music. Herbert Kretzmer said: "Writing a theme song is no easy task. The first verse could only run for 35 seconds, the time before the play began. It also had to run over the main titles and be complete in itself. Then it had to be stretched out to a record, so that it did not sound like padding. At the time, Aznavour was touring all over the place and it took some time to get a melody from him. The moment he played me that long, opening note, the word *She* jumped into my mind and I knew we had the song." *She* became an international hit and Aznavour recorded it in several languages. Elvis Costello revived the song in 1999 for the soundtrack of the film *Notting Hill*. It is featured over the film's closing credits.

Top of the Pops in 1974

There were 22 number one records in 1974 in the UK single charts published by the NME. The best selling single of the year was *Tiger Feet* by Mud. Second was *Seasons In The Sun* by Terry Jacks. Third was *Billy Don't Be A Hero* by Paper Lace. The biggest selling album of the year was *The Singles: 1969-1973* by The Carpenters. Below is a table of the Number One singles through the year of 1974.

Merry Xmas Everybody
Slade
From 15th Dec 1973 for 5 weeks

You Won't Find Another Fool Like Me
The New Seekers
From 19th Jan 1974 for 1 week

Tiger Feet
Mud
From 26th Jan 1974 for 4 weeks

Devil Gate Drive
Suzi Quatro
From 23rd Feb 1974 for 2 weeks

Jealous Mind
Alvin Stardust
From 9th Mar 1974 for 1 week

Billy Don't Be A Hero
Paper Lace
From 16th Mar 1974 for 3 weeks

Seasons In The Sun
Terry Jacks
From 6th Apr 1974 for 4 weeks

Waterloo
ABBA
From 4th May 1974 for 2 weeks

Sugar Baby Love
The Rubettes
From 18th May 1974 for 4 weeks

The Streak
Ray Stevens
From 15th Jun 1974 for 1 week

Always Yours
Gary Glitter
From 22nd Jun 1974 for 1 week

She
Charles Aznavour
From 29th Jun 1974 for 4 weeks

Rock Your Baby
George McCrae
From 27th Jul 1974 for 3 weeks

When Will I See You Again
The Three Degrees
From 17th Aug 1974 for 2 weeks

Love Me For A Reason
The Osmonds
From 31st Aug 1974 for 3 weeks

Kung Fu Fighting
Carl Douglas
From 21st Sep 1974 for 3 weeks

Annie's Song
John Denver
From 12th Oct 1974 for 1 week

Sad Sweet Dreamer
Sweet Sensation
From 19th Oct 1974 for 1 week

Everything I Own
Ken Boothe
From 26th Oct 1974 for 3 weeks

Gonna Make You A Star
David Essex
From 16th Nov 1974 for 3 weeks

You're The First, The Last, My Everything
Barry White
From 7th Dec 1974 for 2 weeks

Lonely This Christmas
Mud
From 21st Dec 1974 for 4 weeks

Canadian philosopher Marshall McLuhan once famously said that: "Art is anything you can get away with." In 1974, Serbian performance artist Marina Abramović took this to extremes and nearly didn't get away with it. Her, *Rhythm 0* show in Naples, Italy involved 72 objects being laid out on a table. These ranged from benign things like a feather, some perfume, honey, a rose and some wine, to altogether more sinister objects such as a scalpel, scissors, a metal bar, nails and a gun and a bullet. Her instructions to the audience were that the objects on the table could be used on her as they desired, stating: "I am the object, during this period. I take full responsibility." The show was scheduled to last six hours, during which time the audience split into two groups, those seeking to attack her and those fighting off the aggressors.

Artist Marina Abramović

New World Cup trophy

She survived, but claims never to have fully recovered from the experience. Probably the most viewed sculpture of the year was the new FIFA football World Cup trophy. The previous Jules Rimet trophy had been awarded outright to Brazil in 1970, when they won their third World Cup. Italian sculptor Silvio Gazzaniga was commissioned to make a new trophy. He explained his thoughts behind the design: "The lines spring out from the base, rising in spirals, stretching out to receive the world. From the remarkable tensions of the compact body of the sculpture rise the figures of two athletes at the stirring moment of victory." Over 75,000 people were at the Olympic Stadium in Munich to witness West German captain Franz Beckenbauer hold the cup aloft. Hundreds of millions worldwide watched it on television. The Nobel Prize in literature was awarded jointly to Eyvind Johnson and Harry Martinson. Eyebrows were raised as Johnson had been a member of the judging panel until 1972. In a rather clunky statement, the committee said that the decision was "fairly unanimous." Others on the shortlist were Graham Greene and V.S. Naipal. Greene was never awarded the prize, but Naipal won it in 2001. On 12th February 1974, author Aleksandr Solzhenitsyn was arrested for treason for his 1973 book *Gulag Archipelago*. Having previously incarcerated him and attempted to poison him, the Soviet authorities decided to deport the 1970 Nobel Prize winner. Safe passage was negotiated by KGB chief Yuri Andropov and West German Chancellor Willy Brandt. Solzhenitsyn was then free to work as he wished in the west. In November, the comedian Max Wall took to the stage at the Greenwich Thetre in London. John Osborne had written the play *The Entertainer* in 1956 about a faded, jaded music hall star. Osborne was unhappy with the original casting stating that: "The original production was unfortunately overshadowed by the presence and performance of Laurence Olivier." So, 17 years after its debut, he decided to direct the play himself, casting the man who many speculated was the inspiration for lead character Archie Rice. Frank Marcus, writing in the Telegraph, agreed with Osborne when he wrote: "The one and only Max Wall takes less than 30 seconds to make Olivier look like an amateur. Here is conclusive proof that a lifetime's experience in music hall cannot be imitated by a 'straight' actor."

Comedian Max Wall

Carrie

Author: Stephen King   Published: 5th April 1974

Stephen King's debut novel tells the haunting story of Carietta 'Carrie' White, a shy and socially awkward high school girl with telekinetic powers. Bullied by her classmates and abused by her fanatically religious mother, *Carrie* struggles to navigate her tumultuous adolescence. The narrative unfolds as *Carrie* discovers her telekinetic abilities and begins to explore their extent, using them both defensively and destructively. The novel reaches its climax during the high school prom, where Carrie's peers subject her to a cruel prank, triggering a cataclysmic display of her powers that culminates in a tragic bloodbath. Through Carrie's story, King explores themes of isolation, trauma and the consequences of unchecked cruelty. Carrie remains a seminal work in the horror genre, showcasing King's talent for crafting deeply unsettling tales that resonate with readers long after they've turned the final page.

If Beale Street Could Talk

Author: James Baldwin   Published: 17th June 1974

Baldwin delves into the lives of African Americans living in Harlem during the 1970s. The story revolves around Tish, a young woman deeply in love with her childhood friend, Fonny. However, their happiness is shattered when Fonny is falsely accused of rape and imprisoned. Despite the injustice they face, Tish and Fonny's families unite to fight for his freedom. Baldwin's novel skilfully examines the complexities of racism, poverty and the criminal justice system, all the while emphasising the resilience and strength of the human spirit. Through lyrical prose and vivid characterisations, Baldwin captures the essence of Harlem, portraying both its vibrancy and its struggles. Baldwin's narrative weaves a tapestry of love, resilience and injustice, portraying the energetic yet turbulent landscape of Harlem. Through poignant prose the book serves as a testament to the enduring power of hope, and the quest for dignity amidst oppression.

Tinker, Tailor, Soldier, Spy

Author: John le Carré   First published in June 1974

Set during the Cold War era, the story follows retired intelligence officer George Smiley as he is brought back to uncover a Soviet mole within the highest echelons of the British Secret Intelligence Service (MI6). As Smiley delves into the intricate web of deception and betrayal within the intelligence community, he navigates a labyrinth of suspicion and double-crossing, all the while grappling with his own personal demons. Le Carré's masterful storytelling and meticulous attention to detail create a gripping narrative that immerses readers in the shadowy world of espionage and intrigue. The book is celebrated for its complex characters, atmospheric setting and layered plot, cementing its status as a classic of the spy genre. Its exploration of loyalty, betrayal and the cost of duty make it a timeless and compelling read. George Smiley has been portrayed many times on screen, but for most people he will forever be associated with Alec Guinness.

Porterhouse Blue
Author: Tom Sharpe   First published in 1974

Porterhouse College is world renowned for its gastronomic excellence, the arrogance of its fellows, its academic mediocrity and the social cache it confers on the athletic sons of country families. It is a Cambridge college held fast by the steel cobwebs of tradition. It is famous for rowing and low academic standards. What Porterhouse needs is money. Therefore, they will take any wealthy student whether or not that student knows how to put his shoes on the right feet. Sir Godber Evans, ex-Cabinet Minister and the new Master, is determined to change all of this. Spurred on by his politically ambitious wife, Lady Mary, he challenges the established order and provokes the wrath of the Dean, the Senior Tutor, the Bursar and most intransigent of all, Skullion the Head Porter. The author attended Pembroke College, Cambridge and his inside knowledge of Oxbridge affairs is brilliantly satirised.

The Conservationist
Author: Nadine Gordimer   Booker Prize Winner in 1974

The book opens with an unidentified dead black man found face down near a river that runs through a farm called Mehring's Willows. No one knows him and the police don't even bother to investigate the death. The book mostly follows the interior monologue of Mehring, a wealthy white colonial industrialist in South Africa, who has bought the farm. His farm is managed by a group of extremely poor black people, lead by Jacobus, who all seem to have infinite patience. Mehring's life is so removed from theirs that he barely empathises with them at all. He has also grown distant from the members of his own class who spend their spare time partying and trying to fix him up with single eligible women. This Booker Prize winning novel serves as a metaphor for Apartheid South Africa, where a privileged class are slowly seeing their society collapse around them and a black underclass still seeing emancipation as a distant dream.

All the President's Men
Written By Carl Bernstein and Bob Woodward   Published: 15th June 1974

The book is a riveting detective story, capturing the exhilarating rush of the biggest presidential scandal in US history. It is as, former *New York Times* managing editor, Gene Roberts has called it: "Maybe the single greatest reporting effort of all time". It gives a full account of the Watergate scandal from the two *Washington Post* reporters who broke the story. *Time Magazine* called it: "The work that brought down a presidency; perhaps the most influential piece of journalism in history." Published just two months before President Nixon's resignation, *All the President's Men* revealed the full scope of the Watergate scandal and introduced for the first time the mysterious "Deep Throat". Beginning with the story of a burglary at Democratic headquarters and then continuing through headline after headline, the authors deliver the stunning revelations and pieces in the Watergate puzzle that brought about Nixon's shocking downfall.

The Last of the Really Great Whangdoodles
Author: Julie Andrews Edwards   Published in 1974

The actress Julie Andrews wrote this book under her married name. She had starred as Mary Poppins in 1965 and brings elements of that experience to this story. The Whangdoodle was once the wisest, kindest and most extraordinary creature in the world. Then he disappears and creates a magical land for himself including other remarkable animals: the ten-legged Sidewinders, the little furry Flukes, the friendly Whiffle Bird and the treacherous 'oily' Prock. The Whangdoodle ruled his kingdom all but forgotten by people. But not completely forgotten. Professor Savant believes in the Whangdoodle. When he tells the three Potter children of his search for the spectacular creature, Lindy, Tom and Ben are eager to reach Whangdoodleland. With the Professor's help, they discover a secret way in. But waiting for them was the scheming Prock, who will use almost any means to keep them away from his beloved king.

A Great Day for Up!
Written by Theodor Seuss Geisel aka Dr. Seuss   Published: 28th August 1974

Dr. Seuss' books are known for their lively and inventive use of language, making them an excellent tool for building vocabulary and reading skills in children. With made-up words and clever rhymes, they encourage children to think creatively about language in a way that is both fun and educational. This was the first book in the series not to be illustrated by Geisel himself. Instead he enlisted the help of Quentin Blake who had already illustrated books by Roald Dahl and Sylvia Plath among others. *A Great Day for Up!* is a fun poetry book about the word 'up'. Blake fills it to the brim with with colourful, expressive characters. The vast diversity of subject matter draws readers young and old into the story. These range from kites to mountain climbing, animals, hot air balloons, etc. As the poem progresses, the characters begin to snowball into larger and larger groups that completely fill the pages. (note: image is illustrative)

The Chocolate War
Author: Robert Cromier   First published in 1974

The novel focuses on Jerry Renault who is one of the freshmen at Trinity School, an all-male Catholic preparatory high school. Jerry is a quiet, reserved boy, silently coping with the recent death of his mother and a distant father. Jerry struggles with trying to understand who he is. He experiences all the pains and tribulations of being a teenager. Everything seems to be going well. He is recruited by the school's football team, where he makes a new friend. One day, Jerry is approached by Archie Costello, a representative of The Vigils: Trinity's secret society. The Vigils specialise in creating 'assignments' for new students, which range from simple jokes to cruel, elaborate pranks. Refusing to sell chocolates in the annual school fund-raiser may not seem a radical thing to do. But when Jerry challenges the secret society, his defiant act turns into an all-out war. Now the only question is: Who will survive?

John Kani (pictured in 2015)

Sizwe Banzi Is Dead

Written by and starring John Kani and Winston Ntshona, with Athol Fugard
London Theatre Critics Award for the Best Play of 1974
Played at the Royal Court Theatre and then the Ambassadors Theatre

The play begins in Styles' photographic studio and much of the first scene is ad-libbed. He describes how he previously worked in the Ford Motor Company where he and his fellow black workers had to meticulously clean the plant ahead of a visit by Henry Ford Jr. The plant is spotlessly clean, but Ford looks around for two seconds and walks out. Into Styles' studio walks Sizwe Bansi, a man dressed in his Sunday best, who wants to send a photo home to his wife to show her how well he is doing. In reality he isn't doing well at all, After the photo shoot, the two men go out and get drunk and then stumble across a dead man who they find out from his passbook is called Robert Zwelinzima. Sizwe's problem is that his passbook does not allow him to work legally in Port Elizabeth, but the passbook of Robert Zwelinzima would.

Sizwe is reluctant to assume a dead man's identity, but Styles eventually persuades him by telling him that the passbook system has already stripped him of his humanity and he switches the photos in the books. The play ends with Styles taking photographs of "Robert Zwelinzima", pipe in mouth and a newspaper tucked under his arm, to send back to his wife. As he walks towards the camera Styles says "smile Robert, smile."

Playwright Tom Stoppard

Travesties

Written by Tom Stoppard
Starring John Wood, John Hurt, Tom Bell and Frank Windsor
Premiered on 10th June 1974 at The Aldwych Theatre. London.

The play, set in Zurich during World War I, interweaves the lives of three significant figures of the time: James Joyce, Vladimir Lenin and Tristan Tzara, the founder of the Dada movement. The main protagonist, Henry Carr, serves as the British consul in Zurich and becomes entangled in the lives of these historical figures who were all in the city at the same time. Stoppard spins this historical coincidence into a masterful and riotously funny play, a speculative portrait of what a meeting of these profoundly influential men in a changing Europe might have been like, as seen through the lucid, lurid, faulty but wholly riveting memory of an ageing Carr. The play is a comedy of ideas, blending farce, wordplay and intellectual debate. Stoppard explores the nature of art, politics and revolution through the interactions of these characters. Henry Carr's memories are unreliable and he frequently confuses or misremembers events, adding to the chaotic and absurd atmosphere of the play. Through Carr's encounters with Joyce, Lenin and Tzara, Stoppard examines the clash of ideologies and the breakdown of communication. Joyce is obsessed with his work on Ulysses, Lenin is focused on revolutionary politics and Tzara espouses the nihilistic principles of Dadaism. Their discussions touch on themes of creativity, censorship and the meaning of art in a tumultuous world. *Travesties* is celebrated for its wit, intelligence and theatrical inventiveness.

Monty Python Live at Drury Lane!

Theatre Royal, Drury Lane
26th February to 23rd March, 1974
A live album was released on 24th June 1974

Terry Gilliam

Following on from their hit television series, Michael Palin, Graham Chapman, John Cleese, Eric Idle, Terry Jones and Terry Gilliam took the Monty Python troupe to the West End Stage. The show was a huge success and an initial two-week run was extended to a month, with each show playing to sell-out crowds of 2,200. The show included guest performers such as Neil Innes and Idle's wife Lyn Ashley. The Python team certainly gave the punters what they wanted; the play was filled with old favourites such as *The Lumberjack Song*, *Four Yorkshiremen*, *Nudge Nudge* and *The Dead Parrot Sketch*. Terry Jones described just how big an undertaking the show was performing on a stage where Lerner and Loewe's *Camelot* had opened a year earlier. "It was initially a nerve-wracking proposition, but at the same time it was somehow reassuring to find ourselves part of the 'theatrical establishment' even if it was an illusion." When the show transferred to America, there were subtle differences. In their New York, *Live! At City Center* (1976) performance they featured mock blues and protest songs. Their best parody came with the Beatles mockumentary *All You Need is Cash* (1978), which was written by Eric Idle and featured Michael Palin, Bianca Jagger and a self deprecating George Harrison. Americans Dan Aykroyd and Bill Murray also guested.

John, Paul, George, Ringo..... & Bert

Written by Willy Russell
Premiered at The Everyman Theatre, Liverpool in May 1974
Winner of the Evening Standard Best Musical Award

Bernard Hill starred as John Lennon

In conversation with actor John Bennett, Willy Russell revealed his motivation for writing the musical. He explained that back then Liverpool had completely and utterly turned its back on The Beatles after their spilt. There was no idea at the time that they would ever become this massive cultural feature of Liverpool life, even though the Beatles had been a huge phenomenon. The Beatle thing had happened and now they were dead and gone. The city was full of men propping up bars, claiming to have worked with the Fab Four. It was in that atmosphere that Russell was approached to write the play, *John, Paul, George, Ringo... & Bert*. It told the story of The Beatles from their formation to a fictional reunion through the eyes of the narrator Bert McGhee, a warehouse worker who claimed to have been part of the group in the days of The Quarrymen until he confused an A minor chord with a G seventh.

The original cast saw Bernard Hill playing John and Trevor Eve playing Paul. The music was largely performed by Barbara Dickson. Just as the Beatles propelled Liverpool onto the international music stage, Russell was instrumental in creating a theatrical culture which nurtured young, local talent, most notably when he cast Julie Walters in the RSC commissioned *Educating Rita* (1980).

This example is situated in Santa Cruz, Tenerife

British sculptor Henry Moore in 1973

Goslar Warrior

Created by Henry Moore in 1973 - 1974

Henry Moore created seven casts of this giant bronze statue measuring over 3 metres (10 feet). Two of the casts are on public display, including the one above. The other is in the gardens of the Imperial Palace of Goslar in Goslar, Germany.

The sculpture is located on Mathew Street in the Cavern Quarter of Liverpool

Liverpudlian sculptor Arthur Dooley
(image courtesy of Writing on the Wall)

Four Lads Who Shook the World

Created by Arthur Dooley in 1974

An iconic photograph opportunity for enthusiastic Beatles fans directly opposite the legendary Cavern Club, this sculpture by renowned Liverpool artist and sculptor Arthur Dooley depicts the Madonna surrounded by the initials of John, Paul, George and Ringo.

A Passion for Churches

Written by Sir John Betjeman   **First broadcast on 7th December 1974 on BBC2**

Following on from his 1973 exploration of London suburbia in the highly acclaimed documentary *Metro-Land*, Poet Laureate Sir John Betjeman embarked on a project very close to his heart. In 1974, the renowned poet and broadcaster captivated audiences with his TV documentary, *A Passion for Churches*. The opening scenes show him aboard a boat on the River Bure. He recalls being eight or nine years old when, on a similar trip with his parents, he saw the outline of a church tower against the sky. That, he explains, was the beginning of his passion for churches. Through this programme, Betjeman embarks on a heartfelt exploration of England's ecclesiastical architecture, delving into the rich history and spiritual significance embodied by its churches. His journey provides viewers with a visual

Sir John Betjeman

feast, as he traverses the 'big sky' landscapes of East Anglia, stopping at various churches that span centuries of architectural evolution. With his trademark wit and charm, he shares his profound admiration for these sacred spaces, each bearing the imprint of its time and community. Throughout the documentary, Betjeman celebrates the diverse architectural styles that define England's churches, from the grandeur of medieval cathedrals to the humble beauty of rural parish churches. He marvels at the intricate stonework, soaring

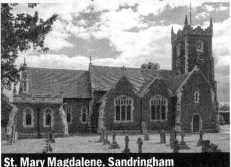
St. Mary Magdalene, Sandringham

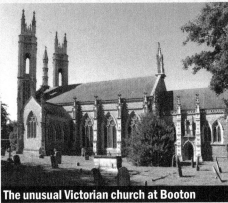
The unusual Victorian church at Booton

spires and luminous stained glass windows that adorn these buildings, showcasing the craftsmanship and devotion of generations past. However, Betjeman's exploration extends beyond mere aesthetics; he also reflects on the social and cultural significance of churches within English society. He discusses their role as centres of community life, places of worship and repositories of local history and tradition. Through his insightful commentary, Betjeman invites viewers to contemplate the enduring relevance of these sacred spaces in an ever-changing world. Moreover, *A Passion for Churches* is imbued with Betjeman's personal reflections and anecdotes, adding an intimate dimension to the documentary. His genuine affection for these architectural marvels shines through as he shares his own experiences and encounters with England's churches, evoking a sense of nostalgia and reverence. Churches featured include: The Church of St. Mary Magdalene at Sandringham, The Rectory at the wonderfully named Great Snoring and Walsingham Abbey. A book also called *A Passion for Churches* was released and people still use it as a travel guide when exploring the fascinating history of our ecclesiastical past.

The Discovery of Sagittarius A*

Sagittarius A* (also known as Sgr A*) is a supermassive black hole located at the centre of our Milky Way galaxy, roughly 26,000 light-years from Earth. Its discovery in 1974 was a pivotal moment in astronomy, providing the first substantial evidence for the existence of black holes. The discovery was made by astronomers Bruce Balick and Robert Brown using the Green Bank Telescope in West Virginia, USA. They detected a strong radio source in the constellation Sagittarius, which they named Sagittarius A*. This source was found to be extremely compact and intense, indicating a highly concentrated mass. Sgr A* is immensely massive, containing about 4.3 million times the mass of our Sun. Its presence is inferred from the orbits of stars near the galactic centre, which move at incredibly high velocities, suggesting a powerful gravitational force. An interesting fact about Sgr

Sagittarius A* imaged by the Event Horizon Telescope, with lines overlaid to mark the orientation of polarisation of the magnetic field

A* is that it remains relatively quiet compared to other active galactic nuclei, emitting less radiation. However, it occasionally flares up, emitting bursts of X-rays and infrared radiation. These flares provide valuable insights into the properties and behaviour of black holes. The study of Sgr A* has significantly advanced our understanding of black holes, galaxy formation, and the dynamic processes at the core of galaxies. It continues to be a focal point of astronomical research, with ongoing observations aiming to unravel more of its mysteries.

The Arecibo Message

The Arecibo message, sent on 16th November 1974, was a landmark event in the search for extraterrestrial intelligence. Crafted by a team led by astronomer Frank Drake, with contributions from Carl Sagan, it was transmitted from the Arecibo Observatory in Puerto Rico. The observatory, equipped with a 305-meter radio telescope, was one of the most powerful and sensitive in the world at that time. The message was a binary-encoded signal, designed to convey basic information about humanity and our planet. It consisted of 1,679 bits, which, when arranged into a 23 by 73 grid, depicted several key elements: the numbers one to ten, the atomic numbers of essential elements (hydrogen, carbon, nitrogen, oxygen, and phosphorus), the formulas for the sugars and bases in DNA, a graphic of the DNA double helix, a figure of a human with physical dimensions, a diagram of the Solar System indicating Earth, and a representation of the Arecibo telescope. This message was aimed at the globular star cluster M13, located approximately 25,000 light-years away. Although it was more of a symbolic gesture to demonstrate human technological capabilities rather than a genuine attempt at communication, the message will take 25,000 years to reach its target, and any reply would take an equivalent amount of time to return.

Left: A colourised section of the message to more easily identify the constituent elements

Skylab

It was back in the early 1950s that German-born rocket engineer Wernher von Braun published a series of articles entitled *Man Will Conquer Space Soon* envisioning a space station. At that time, author Arthur C. Clarke also predicted that a space station would be an important early step in space exploration. The opportunity for NASA to actually build and deploy such a station came as a result of an accident in the Apollo space program. In 1970, Apollo 13 took off on-board a Saturn V rocket for what would become an infamous mission where the crew had an extraordinary escape after an accident on-board mid-flight. Consequently, the planned Apollo 18 and 19 missions were cancelled. The idea was then proposed to re-purpose one of the remaining Saturn V's into a space

The Skylab space station in orbit, as photographed by departing crew in 1974

station by converting the third stage of the rocket into a laboratory and living quarters. After three years of testing and development, the pioneering United States space station, Skylab, launched on 14th May 1973. It pushed the boundaries of human exploration and redefined our understanding of living and working in space. The station featured a spacious living area, a scientific workshop, and a solar observatory. It demonstrated remarkable ingenuity and adaptability in converting existing space hardware. Between May 1973 and February 1974, three different crews were sent to Skylab totalling about 24 weeks of occupation. The crew of Skylab, a mix of astronauts, engineers and scientists, embarked on a series of ground-breaking experiments. Their studies of prolonged space habitation on the body were instrumental in understanding the challenges of long-duration space missions and designing countermeasures to mitigate potential health risks. The Apollo Telescope Mount, a sophisticated observatory aboard Skylab, captured high-resolution images of the sun revealing its intricate structure and shedding light on solar flares and coronal mass ejections. The crew also photographed and documented our planet, contributing to our knowledge of weather patterns, land forms, and environmental changes. Life aboard Skylab wasn't all work and no play. Astronauts delighted in testing the limits of micro gravity from flying like Superman through the modules to inventing a zero-gravity coffee cup. The station suffered a major setback when its sun shield was damaged during launch, causing excessive heat inside. The resourceful crew fashioned a makeshift parasol using a sunshade from inside the

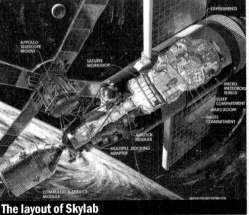

The layout of Skylab

station and a pole from a telescoping cleaning tool. When the Skylab 4 crew left in February 1974, it was expected that the Skylab 5 mission would bring a further crew. However, this mission was cancelled. As Skylab was in a low earth orbit, gravity was slowly pulling it back towards the planet. NASA hoped that the Space Shuttle programme would be ready in time to allow a mission to thrust Skylab into a higher orbit. Unfortunately, the shuttle was not ready in time. And so, on 11th July 1979 the station re-entered Earth's atmosphere, disintegrating into a fiery spectacle over the Indian Ocean. Its legacy lives on, as Skylab paved the way for future space stations like the International Space Station.

A view of the Expo '74 site including the Great Northern Clocktower

preserve the environment

EXPO'74

"The Earth does not belong to man, man belongs to the Earth."
A simple idea, reputedly an Indian chief's answer to settlers who wanted to buy the land where his people lived. But it took more than 100 years for most men to realize the full dimension of that truth and the consequences of ignoring it.
Now it is an idea whose time has come—too late, many say, man has built an affluent civilization only to find that he has permanently upset the balance of nature on which his survival depends. But few accept that dismal view, and the effort to restore the balance has begun. It is barely underway, but hope is quickening that the balance not only will be restored but preserved forever. Out of this hope and effort comes the first environmental world's fair.

Expo '74—'Celebrating Tomorrow's Fresh, New Environment'.

Spokane, Washington, is in the center of one of the last areas of unspoiled natural beauty left on earth—the American and Canadian Pacific Northwest—is the site of this celebration of nature's promise to man and man's promise to her. It will be remembered as the place the start was made.

The Expo '74 stamp is an original design by artist Peter Max. His "Cosmic Jumper" strides through a rainbow universe of sunlight, clouds, earth and water, circled by flying birds, under the gaze of the "Smiling Stags". The original engravings were executed between 1870 and 1906.

Stamps printed by the Bureau of Engraving and Printing, Washington, D.C.

Copyright 1974 American Bank Note Company

No. 28 in a series

April 18, 1974 / Printed in U.S.A.

Commemorative stamps produced for the Expo

Expo '74, officially known as the International Exposition on the Environment was held in Spokane, Washington, from 4th May to 3rd November 1974. It was the first world's fair dedicated to environmental issues. World expos, or world's fairs, are large international exhibitions designed to showcase the achievements of nations and foster global unity and progress. The tradition dates back to the Great Exhibition of 1851 in London, and over the years, expos have introduced innovations such as the telephone, the Ferris wheel, and the Space Needle. Expo '74 was innovative for its environmental focus, reflecting growing global awareness of ecological concerns during the early 1970s. The event's theme, 'Celebrating Tomorrow's Fresh New Environment', highlighted the importance of environmental stewardship and sustainable living. Spokane was chosen as the host city due to its efforts to rejuvenate its downtown area, particularly the Spokane River and its adjacent industrial sites. The fair transformed the previously polluted riverfront into a vibrant park, showcasing the potential for urban environmental restoration. Riverfront Park, the heart of Expo '74, was created by removing old railroad yards and re-purposing the area into a green space that remains a central feature of Spokane today.

Although mired in the Watergate scandal, President Richard Nixon officially opened the fair setting the stage for six months of exhibitions, events, and attractions. Expo '74 featured pavilions from over 50 nations and numerous corporations. Highlights included the US and USSR Pavilions, which showcased each countries environmental research and achievements. Other attractions included the world's first IMAX Theatre, which featured the then-revolutionary large-format film technology. The fair also featured a working model of the Space Needle from the 1962 Seattle World's Fair and an environmental art exhibit called 'The Magic of a People's Theatre'. The fair revitalised the city, leaving behind a legacy of urban renewal and environmental consciousness. Riverfront Park remains a cherished public space, housing remnants of the fair such as the Looff Carousel, the Great Northern Clocktower and many sculptures. The most famous of these is the *Garbage Goat* created by the 'welding nun' Sister Paula Mary Turnbull. Other structures, including the Republic of China pavilion were moved 150 miles to form classrooms and a performance theatre for the Walla Walla community college. The success of Expo '74 also demonstrated that smaller cities could effectively host world-class events, paving the way for future expos in less traditional locations.

The Sinclair Scientific

In 1972 in the USA, Hewlett Packard introduced the the HP-35. It was the world's first scientific pocket calculator that could use trigonometric and exponential functions. However, it was extremely expensive at $395 (around £165). Back over in Cambridge, UK, Clive Sinclair was determined to launch a rival calculator at a much lower price. Utilising a single microchip from Texas instruments, Sinclair's colleague Nigel Searle was able to design algorithms that allowed scientific functions to be performed at the cost of speed and some accuracy. However, this breakthrough design allowed a significantly cheaper calculator to be produced. The Sinclair Scientific was launched in 1974 in the UK at a price of £49.95. Powered by 3 x AAA batteries and with a Light Emitting Diode screen the Sinclair Scientific proved extremely popular. Further relentless work in reducing the cost of manufacture meant that by July 1976, the public could purchase one of these calculators for only £7, a seventh of the original launch price and over 20 times cheaper than the HP-35. The Sinclair Scientific was followed up in August 1975 by the Sinclair Scientific Programmable. It included 24-step programming capabilities and a library of over 120 programmes that could perform common mathematical operations.

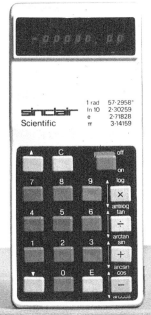

The Sinclair Scientific calculator

The Honeywell Page Printing System

In 1974, the Honeywell corporation of America announced the launch of its ground breaking Page Printing System. During the 1970s as computing permeated the workplace, the requirement to both store and print huge amounts of data and documents grew at a steep rate. Traditional printing technology had failed to keep up with the demand for high speed solutions. This was in part due to the technological limitations of 'impact' printers. These are machines that physically strike the paper or strike an inked ribbon on to paper. Examples of these included the teleprinter, daisy wheel printers and dot matrix printers. The innovation which

Changing the paper roll of the Honeywell PPS

unblocked the logjam was electrostatic printing. This is a non contact form of printing where a chemically coated paper is charged electrostatically by a print head. The charged areas of the paper attract the ink and thereby create the image. The Honeywell PPS used this technologically to create a printer capable of printing 18,000 lines per minute; that's the equivalent of 10 pages per second. With this colossal speed the paper needed to be supplied in perforated rolls as opposed to individual sheets. With the ability to print 600 pages per minute the rolls needed to be very long. In fact, the standard roll of paper was almost ¾ mile long. Companies such as NASA, BP Oil and Massey Ferguson were early customers.

The Sikorsky UH-60 Black Hawk

The UH-60 Black Hawk helicopter, developed by Sikorsky Aircraft, made its first flight on 17th October 1974. Designed as a versatile and reliable medium-lift utility helicopter, it was introduced to replace the iconic UH-1 Iroquois (Huey) in the US Army's fleet. The Black Hawk's design focused on enhanced performance, survivability, and operational versatility. The UH-60 is powered by twin General Electric T700 turbo shaft engines, providing exceptional lift and speed capabilities. It can reach speeds of up to 183 mph and has a range of approximately 370 miles without refuelling. Its robust air frame and advanced rotor system enable it to operate in various environments,

A US Army Black Hawk

from deserts to arctic conditions. It can carry up to 11 fully equipped troops or over 4 tonnes of cargo. The Black Hawk features an armoured fuselage, crash-resistant seats, and redundant flight systems, enhancing crew safety and mission reliability. The helicopter could be fitted with various configurations for different missions, including troop transport, medical evacuation (MEDEVAC), and electronic warfare. It has been deployed in numerous conflicts and humanitarian missions worldwide. Over 4,000 Black Hawks have been built, and it remains a critical asset for military forces globally to this day, proving its effectiveness and versatility in both combat and peacetime operations.

The Eurocopter AS350 Écureuil (aka Astar in North America)

A Squirrel helicopter flying in Italy

The Eurocopter AS350 Écureuil (Squirrel) is a light utility helicopter that first took to the skies on 27th June 1974. Developed by the French company Aérospatiale, which later became part of Airbus Helicopters, the AS350 was designed to be a versatile and high-performance aircraft suitable for a wide range of civilian and military applications. The AS350 features a single-engine design, typically powered by the Turbomeca Arriel engine, which provides exceptional power and reliability in combination with an advanced Starflex main rotor system. This gives the helicopter remarkable high-altitude performance and the ability to operate in extreme conditions, from hot deserts to cold mountains. Its design also includes a spacious cabin that can accommodate up to six passengers and a pilot. This versatility has made it a favourite for numerous roles, including aerial work, law enforcement, emergency medical services (EMS), and tourism. In 2005, pilot Didier Delsalle landed an AS350 B3 on the summit of Mount Everest at 8,848 meters (29,029 feet), setting a world record for the highest-altitude landing. The extremely good visibility from the cabin has made it the most popular helicopter for sightseeing tourism such as tours to the Grand Canyon from Las Vegas. Examples of use for disaster response include the 2010 Chilean earthquake, the 2011 Norway terror attacks, and Australian bush fires where modified helicopters are equipped with bucket and tank systems.

The BAE Systems Hawk

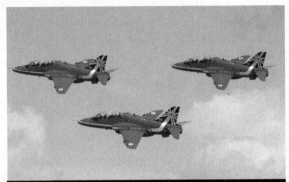

Three Red Arrows Hawk aircraft pictured in 2014

The BAE Systems Hawk is a British single-engine, advanced jet trainer aircraft that first flew on 21st August 1974. Under the control of test pilot Duncan Simpson, the Hawk prototype took off from Dunsfold Aerodrome in Surrey (where latterly the BBC Top Gear series was filmed). Developed by Hawker Siddeley, which later became part of BAE Systems, the Hawk was designed to provide pilot training and serve as a light combat aircraft. The Hawk features a low wing design with a tandem cockpit arrangement, accommodating an instructor and a trainee. It is powered by a Rolls-Royce Adour turbofan engine, delivering reliable performance and efficient fuel consumption. The aircraft's advanced avionics, responsive handling, and high-performance capabilities provide an ideal training platform for transitioning to front-line fighter jets. The Hawk can reach speeds of up to 639 mph and has a range of approximately 1,500 miles. Over 1,000 aircraft have been put into service in more than 18 countries seeing widespread use in training fighter pilots for air forces around the world. The Hawk is most famous for its use by the Royal Air Force's Red Arrows aerobatic display team. Famous for their 'Diamond Nine' flying formation, the Red Arrow's have performed at over 4,800 displays in over 50 countries worldwide.

The General Dynamics F-16 Fighting Falcon

The General Dynamics F-16 Fighting Falcon is a single-engine, multi-role fighter aircraft that first flew on 2nd February 1974. Designed initially as a lightweight air superiority day fighter, it has evolved into an all-weather multi-role aircraft. The F-16 was developed by General Dynamics (now Lockheed Martin) for the United States Air Force (USAF), and it remains one of the most widely used fighter jets globally. The F-16's design incorporates several innovative features, including a frame-less bubble canopy for better visibility, a side-mounted control stick for easier control during high-G manoeuvres, and a

A US Air Force F-16 flying over the desert in 2008

reclined seat to help counteract the effects of G-forces. Its aerodynamic configuration and powerful Pratt & Whitney F100 or General Electric F110 engine allow it to achieve speeds over Mach 2 (1,500 mph or 2,414 km/h). The F-16 is capable of performing various missions, including air-to-air combat, air-to-ground attack, and electronic warfare. The aircraft's agility, advanced avionics, and relatively low operating costs have contributed to its widespread adoption. To date, over 4,600 F-16 aircraft have entered service in over 25 countries. F-16's were widely used over Iraq by the US air force in 1991's Operation Desert Storm. They were also deployed in 1999 for NATO's Operation Allied Force in Kosovo.

The Terracotta Army is Discovered

In 1974, one of the most astounding archaeological discoveries of the 20th century was made in Lintong District, Xi'an, Shaanxi Province, China. It was the unearthing of the Terracotta Army, a vast collection of life-sized clay soldiers buried with the first Emperor of China, Qin Shi Huang, to accompany him in the afterlife. The story begins with a group of local farmers digging a well in the fields near Xi'an. As they dug deeper, they stumbled upon fragments of pottery and bronze. Unbeknownst to them, they had unearthed one of the greatest archaeological finds in history. Archaeologists were quickly alerted to the site and excavations commenced. What they uncovered was breathtaking. Buried beneath the earth lay an army of thousands of intricately crafted clay soldiers, each with unique facial features and expressions. These soldiers were part of a massive funerary complex constructed to guard the tomb of Qin Shi Huang, who ruled China from 221 to 210 BC.

One of the many pits full of soldiers

Many soldiers are depicted on horseback

The army was accompanied by chariots, horses and other figures, all meticulously crafted and arranged in battle formation. It is a testament to the power, wealth and artistic sophistication of ancient China. The sheer scale of the undertaking is staggering, with estimates suggesting that over 8,000 soldiers, 130 chariots and 670 horses were buried near the emperor's tomb. Each terracotta warrior is unique, with individualised facial features, hairstyles and armour, indicating that they were modelled on real soldiers. The discovery of the Terracotta Army has provided invaluable insights into ancient Chinese history, military practices and artistic techniques. It has helped researchers understand the scale and organisation of the Qin Dynasty's military forces and provided clues about the emperor's beliefs regarding the afterlife. The Terracotta Army attracts millions of visitors from around the world each year. In 1987, it was designated a UNESCO World Heritage Site. It is estimated that 700,000 labourers worked for approximately 40 years to complete the terracotta army and tomb complex. The site may yet reveal some grim secrets of the past. Following Emperor Qin Shi Huang's unexpected death in 210 BC, his son decreed that it would be inappropriate for his father's childless concubines to be free, so they were ordered to follow the First Emperor into the grave. Soon after, it was suggested that the artisans responsible for making the tomb's mechanical devices knew too much about the secrets of the treasure hidden inside. Sima Qian, an historian of the early Han Dynasty wrote that "the middle gate was shut and the outer gate closed to imprison all the artisans and labourers, so that not one came out." Trees and grass were then planted over the pyramid-shaped mausoleum to make it look like a hill. Because the 56sq km tomb (around the size of Manhattan Island) is largely unexcavated, and is likely to remain like that for the foreseeable future, the accuracy of Sima Qian's writings cannot be confirmed.

Cyclone Tracy devastates Darwin on Christmas Day

On Christmas Day 1974 a weather event tore Darwin apart, but brought Australia together. While the rest of the country was preparing for the festivities, a ferocious cyclone hit the capital of The Northern Territory. Wind gusts were recorded at 217 km/h before the anemometer was destroyed. Gales extended to about 40 kilometres from the cyclone's centre. 255 mm of rain fell in 12 hours overnight, 145 mm in the two half-hour periods on either side of the eye of the cyclone. There was a storm surge of 1.6 metres in Darwin's harbour; an estimated 4 metres at Casuarina Beach. 71 people were killed, 145 people

A satellite image of Cyclone Tracy

were seriously injured and a further 500 received minor injuries. Around three quarters of the city's houses were left beyond repair. The cyclone crossed the coast near Fannie Bay at around 3.30am on Christmas morning. Had it struck during the daytime, the death toll could have been much higher. Most of those who lost their lives were killed by flying debris or were crushed beneath their houses. In the immediate aftermath of the cyclone, the evacuation of the majority of the population was considered essential given there was no running water, no sanitation, no electricity, little shelter and a high risk of disease outbreaks. More than 36,000

Devastation in the wake of Cyclone Tracy

people left Darwin, filling the planes that had arrived with supplies, equipment and specialised personnel. Voluntary organisations swung into gear, many sending in teams as soon as news of the disaster broke. Many refugees from the Darwin Cyclone were housed by relatives or friends in other parts of Australia, other were put up by kind-hearted fellow citizens. Most of Darwin's population emerged from the cyclone in a state of shock. These days there is a much more sophisticated understanding of the psychological impact of being involved in major disasters, both for those who live through them and for the staff or volunteers who go in afterwards. On 28th February 1975 the Whitlam government established the Darwin Reconstruction Commission, following the Prime Minister's pledge "to make a determined and unremitting effort to rebuild your city and relieve suffering." The Commission's mandate was to reconstruct Darwin within five years. In fact, it achieved this in a little more than three years. It was only then, in the middle of 1978, that Darwin's population reached its pre-cyclone levels. In time, some good would come out of the experience of Cyclone Tracy. The main benefit was the introduction of greatly improved building standards that would apply across the entire country. These included requirements that buildings be clad to protect them against flying debris, and that their roofs be tied to the foundations. When Cyclones Larry and Yasi, both stronger than Tracy, hit Innisfail and Mission Beach on 20th March 2006 and 3rd February 2011 respectively, there were no casualties. Another way the country pulled together was by buying the charity single *Santa Never Made it into Darwin* which won the Australian song of the year award in 1975.

This house was gutted in Nakara, northern suburbs of Darwin

The Disappearance of 'Lucky' Lucan

Lord Lucan, born Richard John Bingham, the 7th Earl of Lucan, was a British aristocrat who became infamous for his mysterious disappearance following the murder of his children's nanny, Sandra Rivett, in 1974. He earned the nickname of 'Lucky Lucan', probably given ironically by his friends at the card table who wanted to flatter a man who was an habitual loser. Bingham was born on 18th December 1934 into an affluent family. He attended Eton College and served in the Coldstream Guards before inheriting the title of Earl of Lucan upon his father's death in 1964. Despite his privileged upbringing, Lord Lucan's life was marred by financial difficulties and a tumultuous marriage. In 1963, Lucan married Veronica Duncan, with whom he had three children. However, their marriage was strained, and they separated in 1972. This eventually led to a bitter custody battle over the children. On the night of 7th November 1974,

Bingham marries Veronica Duncan

a tragic and perplexing event occurred at the Lucan family home in Belgravia, London. Sandra Rivett, the children's nanny, was bludgeoned to death with a lead pipe in the basement of the house. Veronica, who was also attacked but survived, identified her estranged husband, Lord Lucan, as the assailant. However, Lucan himself was nowhere to be found. The events of that fateful night triggered a massive manhunt for Lucan, but he seemed to have vanished without a trace. Despite numerous reported sightings and speculations over the years, his fate remains unknown to this day. Some believe he killed himself, while others speculate that he fled the country and assumed a new identity. Theories surrounding Lucan's disappearance abound, ranging from claims of his involvement with high-stakes gambling circles to conspiracy theories involving his alleged connections to intelligence agencies. However, none of these theories has been substantiated and the truth behind Lord Lucan's disappearance continues to elude authorities. Despite the passage of time, the story of the enigmatic aristocrat who vanished into thin air remains one of the most intriguing unsolved mysteries in British history. Some of the theories are:

1. Former Scotland Yard detective Duncan MacLaughlin claimed in 2003 that Lucan had lived as a hippy, called 'Jungle Barry' in India until his death in 1996.

2. Local residents deep in the New Zealand outback claimed in 2007 that a British ex-pat Roger Woodgate could be Lord Lucan.

3. Philippe Marcq, who was part of the same gambling set as the notorious peer, said one of Lord Lucan's best friends related a gruesome story to him over 40 years ago. He claimed the peer was given a shotgun to shoot himself before his body was fed to a tiger owned by friend John Aspinall at his private zoo in Kent.

Lord Lucan was declared 'dead in absentia', on 27th October 1999, allowing his son George Bingham to assume his titles.

The Life and Death of Oskar Schindler

Oskar Schindler died on the 9th October 1974 in Hildesheim, West Germany at the age of 66. He was born on 28th April 1908 in Zwittau, part of the Austro-Hungarian Empire (now Czech Republic). He is primarily remembered for his remarkable efforts during the Holocaust to save over 1,200 Jews from the horrors of Nazi concentration camps. His life story is one of courage, humanity and moral responsibility. He grew up in a middle-class family and initially pursued a career in business and engineering. He joined the Nazi Party in 1939, hoping to capitalise on the economic opportunities afforded by the party's rise to power. He acquired a factory in Krakow, Poland, which he used to produce enamelware for the German military. However, Schindler soon became horrified by the atrocities committed against Jews and other persecuted groups under Nazi rule. Witnessing the liquidation of the Krakow ghetto and the deportation of its inhabitants to concentration camps deeply affected him. Despite being a member of the Nazi Party and benefiting from its policies, Schindler began to use his position and resources to protect his Jewish workers. In

Oskar Schindler after the war

1944, as the tide of the war turned against Germany, he took extraordinary risks to save as many Jews as possible. He bribed officials, forged documents and even went bankrupt to prevent the closure of his factory, which served as a haven for his workers. By the war's end, he had spent his entire fortune on protecting and providing for his employees, whom he referred to as his "Schindlerjuden" (Schindler Jews). Following the war, he faced financial hardship and personal struggles. He was initially arrested as a Nazi collaborator but was eventually recognised as a Righteous Among the Nations by the Yad Vashem Holocaust Memorial in Israel for his heroic actions. He emigrated to Argentina in 1949 but later returned to Germany, where he lived a relatively obscure life. In the years following his death on 9th October, 1974, Schindler's story gained widespread recognition thanks in part to Thomas Keneally's book *Schindler's Ark* (later adapted into the acclaimed film *Schindler's List* directed by Steven Spielberg). The book and movie brought Schindler's extraordinary acts of courage and compassion to a global audience, ensuring that his legacy would endure as a symbol of resistance against injustice and oppression. Thankfully there were many people like Schindler who baulked at the barbarism of the Nazi regime. Since 1953, Israel's Holocaust memorial, Yad Vashem, has recognised 26,973 people as Righteous Among the Nations. British recipients of the award include the spy Francis Foley and June Haining, who ran a Christian and Jewish boarding school in Hungary. Both enabled thousands to escape. Another hero was American, Master Sergeant Roddie Edmonds, prisoner-of-war at Stalag IX-A. The commander of the camp ordered Edmonds to identify Jewish soldiers under his command. Edmonds responded, "We are all Jews here", and told the commandant that if he wanted to shoot the Jews he would have to shoot all of the prisoners. He then warned the commandant that if he harmed any of his men, he would be prosecuted for war crimes after the conflict ended. The commandant backed down. Edmonds' actions are credited with saving up to 300 Jewish-American soldiers from probable death.

The Rise and Fall of John Stonehouse

During the late 1950s and early 1960s John Stonehouse was a rising star in the Labour Party; there was even mention of him making it to the very top. By 1974 he was finished, stood accused of fraud and was suspected of being a traitor. Born into a political family, his mother was a former mayor and councillor in Southampton and his father was a trade unionist. Stonehouse moved into politics aged 16 when he joined the Labour party. Educated at the London School of Economics, he gained a particular interest in third-world countries, managing the African co-operative society in Uganda between 1952 and 1954. The former RAF pilot, who served from 1944 until 1946, tried unsuccessfully to become an MP in 1950 in the seat of Twickenham and 1951 in Burton, before winning the seat of Wednesbury. But before Stonehouse, who boasted an IQ of 140, got

Stonehouse pictured in 1967

his first big break as a junior minister in 1964, his head had been turned. In 1969, Josef Frolik, an ex-Czech spy who had defected to the US, claimed Stonehouse was being paid by the Czechs. The MP was left fighting for his career but remained calm under questioning by MI5's infamous Cold War officer Charles Elwell, in the presence of Prime Minister Harold Wilson. He was questioned twice, and extensively so, but denied all the allegations. But his reprieve was short lived. When Labour lost the 1970 election to Edward Heath's Conservatives, Stonehouse had an almighty falling out with Wilson. He decided to put his economics degree to good use and turn to the business world. He set up several businesses across the globe, including an investment bank in Bangladesh, but these failed spectacularly. He was left with debts rumoured to be about

Ex-Czech spy Josef Frolik

£800,000. With Wilson still Labour leader, Stonehouse's hopes of a glittering political future were blocked. So he got creative. He used the signature of his secretary-turned-lover Sheila Buckley to forge documents and listed her as a director on the majority of his companies. He planned to fake his own death, before assuming the identity of Joseph Markham, the dead husband of a constituent and running off into the sunset. He spent months planning it and on 20th November 1974 he left a pile of clothes on a Florida beach and vanished. He then flew to Australia, assumed another new identity, that of another dead constituent called Clive Mildoon, and rendezvoused with Miss Buckley. With no idea about his affair, Stonehouse's wife presumed he had indeed drowned. So did most others. It was there that Stonehouse's luck ran out. Police in

Labour leader Harold Wilson

Melbourne who were tipped off that a well spoken Englishman had newly arrived in the city, believed that it might be the fugitive Lord Lucan. He was arrested and interviewed and his story quickly began to unravel as police discovered he'd entered the country on a false passport. He was then extradited to the UK and on 6th August 1976, he was found guilty of 18 counts of fraud, deception and theft and jailed for seven years.

The Watergate Scandal

The Watergate scandal was a political scandal that occurred in 1973, leading to the resignation of President Richard Nixon. It involved a break-in at the Democratic National Committee headquarters at the Watergate office complex in Washington D.C. by members of Nixon's re-election campaign team. The incident led to a chain of events that ultimately revealed a wide range of illegal activities, including obstruction of justice, abuse of power, and political espionage. The Watergate break-in occurred on 17th June 1972, when five men were caught inside the DNC offices. They were arrested and charged with burglary, conspiracy, and wiretapping. At first, the incident was

The Watergate Complex, scene of the break-in

Walkie-talkie used in the break-in

The Senate Watergate hearings in 1973

dismissed as a minor political prank, but subsequent investigations revealed a much larger conspiracy involving high-level officials in the Nixon administration. The investigation into the Watergate scandal was led by two reporters from The Washington Post, Bob Woodward and Carl Bernstein. Through their investigative reporting, they uncovered a vast web of illegal activities, including secret slush funds, illegal wiretapping, and a network of 'plumbers' whose job it was to prevent leaks of classified information. The investigation also revealed that President Nixon had ordered a cover-up of the Watergate break-in, and had authorised illegal payments to the burglars to ensure their silence. In addition, it was discovered that Nixon had installed a secret taping system in the White House, which recorded all conversations in the Oval Office. In August 1974, facing almost certain impeachment and removal from office, President Nixon announced his resignation. He became the first and only US President to resign from office. The Watergate scandal had a profound impact on American politics and society. It shook the public's faith in government and led to a period of cynicism and distrust in the political process. It also led to a series of reforms to improve government transparency and accountability, including the passage of the Ethics in Government Act and the creation of the Office of Government Ethics. In conclusion, the Watergate scandal was a watershed moment in American history, exposing the dangers of unchecked political power and the importance of a free and independent press. It serves as a cautionary tale for future generations, reminding us of the need to remain vigilant and hold our elected officials accountable to the highest standards of ethical conduct.

President Nixon preparing to address the nation on 29th April 1974

The Attempted Kidnap of Princess Anne

Ian Ball, a 26-year-old unemployed labourer, tried to kidnap Princess Anne on 20th March 1974. At just 23 years old, Princess Anne was remarkably courageous throughout the incident and gave the masked kidnapper a curt response. After shooting her security officer, chauffeur and a nearby journalist who tried to help, Ian Ball got into Princess Anne's limo and told her to get out, to which the princess boldly replied: "Not bloody likely". By a stroke of luck, Ron Russell, a former boxer, happened to be driving past. He thought the incident was simply an argument, but when he went over and saw what was going on, he punched Ball in the back of the head and led the Princess to safety. He has said of the incident: "As a 6ft 4in, ex-heavyweight boxer, I decided I was well-placed to defuse the situation. I wanted to prevent this fellow from getting into any more trouble. So I stopped my car and walked towards him." Police Constable Michael Hills arrived on the scene and called for backup but was also shot. Finally, Detective

Princess Anne pictured in 1974

Constable Peter Edmonds chased after Ball, and he was arrested. Speaking about the incident in an interview with Michael Parkinson, Princess Anne said: "He opened the door, and we had a sort of discussion about where or where not we were going to go. He said I had to go with him, can't remember why. I said I didn't think I wanted to go. I was scrupulously polite because I thought it was silly to be too rude or that sort of thing." She added: "We had a fairly low-key discussion about the fact that I wasn't going to go anywhere, and wouldn't it be much better if he moved away, and we'd all forget about it?" After his arrest, Ian Ball was charged with attempted murder and kidnapping and was assessed and diagnosed with schizophrenia. While he apologised for the incident, he pleaded guilty and was sentenced to 41 years in Broadmoor, a high-security psychiatric hospital in Berkshire, and was detained under the Mental Health Act. He told police that he had believed Anne would be an easy target and that he had learned of her movements by phoning the Buckingham Palace press office. He said: "I had thought about it for years... she would have been the easiest. I have seen her riding with her husband." He added to the police: "I have got no friends. I'm a loner. I put a lot of thought and work into it. I can't expect people like you to understand or accept

The Royal limousine involved in the incident

that I did it and planned it alone." In 2002, the Guardian reported Ian had gone on a hunger strike and was referring to himself as a "political prisoner" but aside from this, it was reported that he was a model patient. All the wounded parties in the kidnap attempt recovered and Inspector Beaton was awarded the George Cross by the Queen, while Police Constable Hills and Russell were awarded the George Medal. Chauffeur Callender, McConnell and Edmonds were also awarded the Queen's Gallantry Medal. In 2020, Ron Russell's medal sold for £50.000 at auction.

The Extraordinary Story of Patty Hearst

The story of Patricia Hearst, granddaughter of media magnate William Randolph Hearst, is a tale that captivated America in the 1970s. Patty Hearst's story is one of privilege, radicalisation, kidnapping and ultimately controversy. In February 1974, Hearst, a 19-year-old college student living in Berkeley, California, was kidnapped from her apartment by the Symbionese Liberation Army (SLA), a radical left-wing group. The group demanded a ransom for her release and the distribution of food to the poor in California. However, the Hearst family's attempts to comply with these demands were unsuccessful. During her time in captivity, Patty underwent a dramatic transformation. She soon began to sympathise with her captors' ideology and participated in various criminal activities, including bank robberies, under the name "Tania". This transformation shocked the

Hearst taking part in the Hibernia Bank robbery in April 1974 (CCTV footage)

nation, as the heiress to one of the wealthiest families in America seemingly embraced the cause of her radical kidnappers. In April 1974, Patty was captured alongside several SLA members by law enforcement agents. Despite her claims of being brainwashed and coerced into participating in the group's criminal activities, she was charged with bank robbery and

Patty Heart's police 'mugshot' photos

sentenced to seven years in prison. The case of Patty Hearst raised numerous questions about Stockholm syndrome, a condition first identified in 1973 after a Swedish bank heist. The phenomenon sees hostages develop sympathy for their captors. Many believed that Hearst had willingly joined the group, while others argued that she was a victim of manipulation and coercion. In 1976, President Jimmy Carter commuted Patty Hearst's sentence and she was released from prison after serving only 22 months. She later received a full pardon from President Bill Clinton in 2001. After her release, Patty sought to rebuild her life. She married Bernard Shaw, one of her bodyguards during her trial and had two children. She became involved in philanthropy and writing, publishing a memoir entitled *Every Secret Thing* in 1982, in which she recounted her experiences. The case of Patty Hearst remains one of the most intriguing and controversial chapters in American criminal history. It continues to spark debate about issues such as privilege, coercion and the nature of personal identity. Patty Hearst's journey from heiress to radical to prisoner to free woman is a complex and captivating story that has left an indelible mark on the American consciousness. Hearst's story has featured many times in music, literature and song. American singer-songwriter Patti Smith re-imagined a 1974 cover of Jimi Hendrix's *Hey Joe* as a meditation on Patty Hearst's involvement with the Symbionese Liberation Army. Hall and Oates' *Rich Girl* (1977) was also reputedly inspired by Patty Hearst and in 1988 Natasha Richardson played Hearst in the Paul Schrader directed film *Patty Hearst*. It is interesting to note that a certain Patricia Hearst among the writers!

Hearst being escorted to the courthouse in 1976

Brian Clough

Brian Clough's tenure as the manager of Leeds United in 1974 remains one of the most infamous and shortest-lived episodes in English football history. Clough's arrival at Leeds, following the departure of the highly successful Don Revie, was met with scepticism and controversy from the outset. Clough had gained legendary status as the manager of Derby County, but his outspoken nature and confrontational style clashed with the established culture at Leeds. He criticised the team's aggressive playing style under Revie, famously calling them "dirty" and insinuating they were cheats. His 44-day reign was marked by clashes with players and the board, as he sought to impose his methods on a squad fiercely loyal to their former manager. His abrasive personality alienated key figures within the club, including captain Billy Bremner and influential defender Norman Hunter. Results on the pitch were poor, with only one win in six games, exacerbating tensions within the squad. Clough's insistence on implementing radical changes without understanding the club's culture or players' strengths further undermined his position. Ultimately, Clough was sacked by the Leeds United board after just 44 days in charge, a decision that surprised few given the fevered atmosphere he had created. However, his brief and turbulent stint at Leeds would go down in football folklore, immortalised in book form *The Damned United*, by David Peace (1986) and documentaries as one of the most bizarre managerial appointments in the sport's history. Despite his disastrous spell at Leeds, Clough would go on to achieve further success, notably guiding Nottingham Forest to unprecedented heights, winning back-to-back European Cups in 1979 and 1980 and cementing his legacy as one of English football's most enigmatic and successful managers.

Brian Clough

World Cup Final

The 1974 FIFA World Cup final, held in Munich's Olympiastadion, saw the Netherlands face off against West Germany in a highly anticipated showdown. The Dutch, led by the innovative tactics of Rinus Michels and the mesmerising skills of Johan Cruyff, were considered the favourites. However, the Germans, buoyed by home support and bolstered by the leadership of Franz Beckenbauer, were formidable opponents. The match began explosively, with the Dutch taking the lead in the opening minute through a penalty kick converted by Johan Neeskens. However, the Germans swiftly responded, with Paul Breitner equalising, also from the penalty spot. The decisive moment came in the second half when Gerd Müller, the prolific German striker, netted the winning goal, securing a 2-1 victory for West Germany. The triumph marked West Germany's second World Cup title, solidifying their status as a footballing powerhouse. For the Netherlands, it was a heartbreaking defeat, as they fell short of claiming their maiden World Cup trophy despite their captivating brand of 'Total Football'. The 1974 final remains a memorable chapter in football history, showcasing the clash of two talented teams and the drama that accompanies the pursuit of global glory on the grandest stage.

The 'Love Match' | Chris Evert and Jimmy Connors

The Brash Basher of Belleville had been occasionally beating his elders for four years, but 1974 was the season when all of young Jimbo's prophecies of dominance came true. Mowing opponents down with his revolutionary two-handed backhand, the 21-year-old bashed his way to the first three Grand Slam wins of his career, at the Australian Open, Wimbledon and the US Open. Most famously, with his merciless demolition of ageing Australian legend Ken Rosewall in the finals, his 6-1, 6-0, 6-1 win in the US Open final was the most lopsided in the tournament's history. It wasn't just the majors where Connors excelled; he went 93-4, the second-highest winning percentage (95.9%) in the Open era, after John McEnroe's in 1984. But '74 would leave the bittersweet taste of "what if" in Connors' mouth. Because Connors had played in the unsanctioned, yet lucrative World Team Tennis that year, he was barred from playing at the French Open. Although it might be fanciful to think that he would have completed the Grand Slam at Roland Garos as a young upstart by the name of Bjorn Borg had burst on the scene. Borg won the first of his six French open titles by beating Spaniard Manuel Orantes 2-6, 6-7, 6-0, 6-1, 6-1, in a gruelling final. At the close of 1974, Chris Evert had become one of only three players (with Margaret Court and Billie-Jean King) to ever win 100 matches in a single season, a record which still stands today. The following year, she was only 6 matches shy of repeating the feat. Also during her mammoth 1974 season, she won 55 consecutive matches, a record which lasted 10 years. And her victories were dizzying. She won Wimbledon in 1974, 1976, and 1981. She won the US Open 6 of 8 years between 1975 and 1982, and at one point won four consecutive titles (1975-1978), becoming the first woman since the 1930's to do so. She won a record 7 French championships beginning with back to back titles in 1974 and 75, and took the Australian Open title in 1982 and 84. But of her 18 Grand Slam singles titles, it was the second one, following the French title, at Wimbledon 1974, that her father would remember the most. Jimmy Evert was at home in America. "There was no live TV in 1974," he recalled "She was to call right after the match. So just about an hour had gone by and the phone rings. I pick it up and I just hear this little voice say, 'I won!' and I was silent. So Chris said, 'Dad, are you alright?' But I was so choked up. Just imagine your 19-year-old daughter calling you from England telling you that she had just won Wimbledon."

Jimmy Connors

Chris Evert

Dominant on the court, Evert and Connors were lovers off it. They were also mixed doubles partners, but the two world number 1s could not replicate their singles form. Their best performance in a Major was reaching the 1974 US Open final where they lost 6-1, 7-6 to the Australian-American duo of Geoff Masters and Pam Teeguarden.

The Lion's Infamous Tour of South Africa
On the cry of "99" it was all for one and one for all

Under the apartheid regime, South Africa had become an international pariah. Many of the British public and their leaders were fundamentally opposed to the tour going ahead, though it did materialise, albeit in fiery circumstances. The Lions were captained by the legendary Willie-John McBride and boasted other revered names among their ranks such as Gareth Edwards, JPR Williams, Phil Bennett, Ian

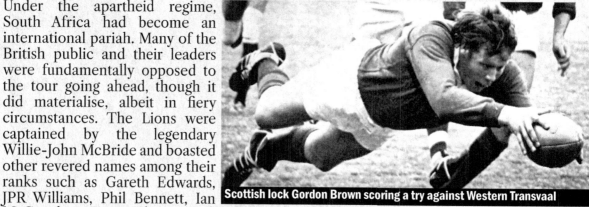

Scottish lock Gordon Brown scoring a try against Western Transvaal

McGeechan, Fergus Slattery and JJ Williams. McBride was well aware of the daunting task ahead of the team, the Springboks had never lost a series on home soil before. It seemed imperative to him that they were all on the same page when he sat his players down before they departed. He said: "I'm going to South Africa...I have one objective: to win the series...it's nothing to do with politics, as far as I'm concerned, nothing. If anybody has any doubt about going on this tour, the door is open. Please leave now." McBride recalled: "Nobody moved. And I said, Okay, we now are on the road." The first significant game of the tour was against Eastern Province, then tough customers in the South African provincial scene. They were led by the Springbok captain Hannes Marais. With the tensions electric off the field, it was inevitable that violence would rear its head on it, and the Lions were prepared. At the shout of McBride's famous "99" call, the men in red swarmed with steely aggression and clenched fists, administering brutal beatings on any opposition player who dared antagonise one of their own. The Lions had made a statement, in no uncertain terms, that their days of being bullied by the burly South Africans were over and the spirit of the tour was forged. The result: Lions 28-14 Eastern Province. The Springboks took on their rivals at a wet and muddy Newlands on the 8th June and were defeated 12-3, the first Lions victory at that venue since 1938. The team bus next pulled up to Loftus Versveld with its occupants in full song belting out *Flower Of Scotland*, sung loudest by Scots lock Gordon Brown, and revelling in a spirit of confidence which manifested on the field of play. The 13th July 1974 saw the sides clash in the vital third test, again, in Port Elizabeth. The Springboks, now desperate for victory, blasted out of the tunnel onto the field like green bullets from a gun, a tongue-lashing from the Minister of Sport in the dressing room still ringing in their ears. What transpired was the most brutal and violent game of the tour. "Fitting more for the boxing ring", a commentator quipped. At the final whistle, the players left the blood-stained pitch with the scoreboard reading 26-9 in the Lion's favour and McBride's men were forever etched in history. The fourth and final test ended in a 13-13 draw, but the writing was already on the wall; that the Springboks had been out-played and out-fought, suffering their first ever home series defeat to a Lions team that would go down as one of the greatest in the tradition. The Lions returned home unbeaten, having played 22 games in all, winning 21 and drawing 1.

"Ashes to Ashes, dust to dust, if Thommo don't get ya, Lillee must"

The night before the first Test of the 1974-75 Ashes series, Dennis Lillee stumbled upon Jeff Thomson sipping quietly on a scotch in a hotel bar. When it was pointed out by his bowling partner that this was an unconventional way to prepare for a game of much magnitude, Thomson's response fizzed like one of his nose-endangering bouncers: "When I go out to bowl, I want the hangover from hell," he said. "I bowl really well when I've got a headache." The great Australian quick must have

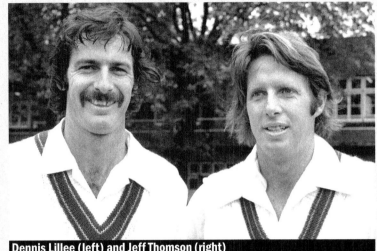

Dennis Lillee (left) and Jeff Thomson (right)

been suffering from the mother 'brown bottle flu' (Australian slang for hangover) that week in Brisbane, if his devastating display against England was anything to go by. The tourists arrived Down Under as underdogs but chipper underdogs, confident following a draw in the West Indies the previous winter and a home drubbing of India. Within five days at the Gabba, between 29th November and 4th December, all optimism had disappeared. The Australian spearheads launched a vicious, relentless, high-velocity assault on England's batsmen, so severe they ended up calling for reinforcements from back home in time for the second Test. Lillee was his usual self, aggressive, determined and never shy to get the top order dancing about their crease, but it was the impact of Thomson that took the English most by surprise. A relative unknown quantity to captain Mike Denness and his team, Thomson had recently relocated to Queensland from his boyhood state of New South Wales. He had played for Australia before, a solitary Test against Pakistan in the winter of 1972-73, but his meagre return from that game (none for 110) hardly set the world on fire. Furthermore his display in a warm-up game against the tourists was erratic. England had nothing to worry about, right? "Just mess around", Chappell told him (he used a stronger word). "Don't show the English batsmen what you can do." Mess around Thomson did and when he was named in the Australia XI for the first Test, English batsman David Lloyd thought there was a typo on the team sheet. It was soon abundantly clear that neither the selectors nor the printers had made a mistake. Thomson opened up with savage pace, peppering the England batsmen as Australia defended their first-innings 309. While England didn't cower first time around, led by a fighting century from Tony Greig, when they returned to the crease for the second innings they had little defence to offer against Thomson and Lillee's undiluted aggression. They crumbled to 166 all out. John Edrich batted with a bruised hand, Dennis Amiss's was broken, Thomson hit Denness so hard in the chest that the England skipper's St. Christopher pendant became lodged in his skin. "He even frightened me sitting in the press box," wrote the former Australia all-rounder Frank Miller. Thomson ripped through the visitors to claim six for 46 in that second innings, taking his match haul to nine for 105. Australia won by 166 runs. Australia won the six match series 4-1.

Red Rum Doubles Up

A winner a record three times in the Grand National, Red Rum is a true Aintree legend. His victories in 1973, 1974 and 1977 cemented his place in Grand National history. Red Rum's association with Aintree began in 1967 when he made his debut appearance in the Thursby Plate race, where he finished in a dead heat with Curlicue. In his first Grand National victory in 1973, Red Rum had to come from behind to beat Australian horse Crisp. In the 1973 race, "Rummy" carried a featherweight of 10st 5lb, in 1974 he was asked to carry the maximum weight of 12st. Many felt that the burden would be too much and he went off at odds of 11-1. But anyone who backed him needn't have worried as he ran to victory leading the field in the closing stages of the race. Later in the 1974 season he would go on to win the Scottish Grand National at Ayr, becoming the only horse to do the 'double'. Red Rum raced again in the 1975 and 1976 Grand Nationals, coming second in 1975 to L'Escargot and second again in 1976 to Rag Trade. Many thought Red Rum's chance of a third victory had passed when he was entered as a 12-year-old in the '77 race. Trainer Ginger McCain had planned the whole season to ensure that Red Rum was at his best for the Grand National. Soon after Becher's Brook 'Rummy' took the lead and won the race to tumultuous applause. Red Rum died on 18th October 1995 at the age of 30 and was laid to rest with his head facing the Aintree winning post.

Red Rum (pictured in 1973)

The Gay Future Affair | An Unsuccessful Coup

What became known as the 'Gay Future Affair' was an ingenious, but ultimately unsuccessful, betting coup that was attempted at Cartmel Racecourse in Cumbria, on Bank Holiday Monday 26th August 1974. Cartmel was chosen because, at the time, it was not connected to the 'Blower' telephone service for bookmakers operated by the Exchange Telegraph Company. Masterminded by Cork construction magnate Tony Murphy, the attempted coup involved two horses, the 'real' Gay Future, who was trained in Tipperary by Edward O'Grady and another four-year-old chestnut gelding, who was sent to permit-holder Tony Collins in Troon, Scotland with counterfeit documents identifying him as Gay Future. Collins was instructed to enter Gay Future in the Ulverston Novices' Hurdle at Cartmel. Two days before the race, the bona fide Gay Future was shipped across the Irish Sea and placed in Collins' charge. Collins was similarly instructed to enter two other horses, Ankerwyke at Southwell and Opera Cloak at Plumpton, although neither was an intended runner. On the morning of the race, Murphy and his associates placed a series of multiple bets on the three Collins-trained runners which, after the withdrawal of Ankerwyke and Opera Cloak, then became single win bets on Gay Future. The horse won easily, by 15 lengths at a generous starting price of 10/1, but bookmakers, smelling a rat, for the most part refused to pay out.

The World Rally Championship

From 1970 to 1972, the precursor to the World Rally Championship (WRC), known as the International Championship for Manufacturers (IMC), was staged across nine international rallies. The inaugural season of the WRC was held in 1973. At this time, trophies were only awarded to manufacturers. Championship awards for drivers and co-drivers were to follow. The 1973 WRC was awarded to Renault with their Alpine A110 dominating the 13-race season. However, things would change dramatically for the 1974 season. For a start, the oil crisis meant that 5 races including the Monte Carlo rally were dropped shortening the season to 8 races. But it was

Renault Alpine A110s dominated in 1973

Team Lancia that shook up the rallying world when they unveiled their Lancia Stratos HF rally car. This is widely regarded as the world's first purpose-built rally car. The mid-engine layout, with a Ferrari Dino V6 engine, provided excellent balance and weight distribution. Its compact, wedge-shaped body, designed by legendary designer Marcello Gandini of Bertone, contributed to its agility and aerodynamic efficiency. To comply with the FIA's Group 4 regulations, Lancia produced 492 road-going versions of the Stratos, ensuring it met the homologation requirements necessary for competition. Whereas 1973 was dominated by the French manufacturer, the '74 season saw a battle between the new Lancia Stratos cars and their Italian compatriots, the Fiat 124 Abarths. Lancia's leading driver was nicknamed 'Il Drago' (The Dragon). Sandro Munari already had a fearsome reputation as a superb driver, but at the controls of the Stratos he would go on to win 3 of the 8 races in '74 season clinching the first in a hat-trick of consecutive manufacturer titles for Lancia.

Lancia's Munari at the wheel of the might Stratos HF

Sandro Munari

Munari at the '74 Rallye Sanremo

The 1974 Formula One World Championship

1973 champion Jackie Stewart did not defend his title in 1974 as he retired at the end of the '73 season. The 1974 title race was closely fought between Brazilian driver Emerson Fitipaldi (McLaren) and Swiss driver Clay Regazzoni (Ferrari). They headed into the last race neck and neck on points. Regazzoni had mechanical problems leaving Fitipaldi to take his second world title. This was also the first time that McLaren claimed the F1 manufacturers title.

The Rumble in the Jungle

On 30th October 1974 in Kinshasa, Zaire

There are similarities between the careers of Muhammed Ali and George Foreman, but also marked differences. Ali, then Cassius Clay, won a gold medal at the 1960 Rome Olympics, as did Foreman in the 1968 Mexico games. There their paths diverge. When Clay was refused service in a restaurant on the grounds of his colour, he reportedly threw his gold medal in the river. Shortly after winning the world crown in 1964, when as underdog he defeated Sonny

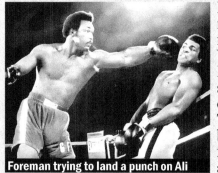

Foreman trying to land a punch on Ali

Liston, Clay joined the Nation of Islam and changed his name to Ali. When Ali was drafted into the US Army to fight in Vietnam he refused, stating that he had no beef with the Viet-Cong and his real enemies lived in America. George Foreman on the other hand held an albeit small stars and stripes aloft when he won gold in Mexico. This was in stark contrast to the Black Power salutes of black Americans Tommie Smith and John Carlos as they collected gold and bronze in the men's 200m at the games. Ali was banned from boxing in 1967 for his act of defiance and was only allowed to return in 1970. His first effort to regain the heavyweight title however failed at the hands of Joe Frazier at Madison Square Garden on 8th March 1971. Billed as the 'Fight of the Century', it was Ali's first professional defeat. Frazier continued to hold the title until 1973 when he lost in a brutal two-round, six-knockdown bout to Foreman. Fast forward to 1974, when Ali took on the all-conquering Foreman in Kinshasa, Zaire (now the Democratic Republic of Congo), in what was billed as 'The Rumble in the Jungle'. The event was packaged and promoted by Don King as a major back-to-Africa cultural event, including a three-day music festival featuring African-American artists James Brown, The Spinners and B.B. King alongside African performers such as Miriam Makeba and Tabu Ley Rochereau. Foreman did not endear himself to the locals when he arrived with his pet Alsatians, a breed which were deployed by the Belgian police during colonial rule. The fight itself was dramatic and entertaining. Foreman was massive favourite. Everyone expected Ali to 'dance' to emphasise movement and footwork, mostly because he'd told everybody so all throughout training camp. Much of the boxing press feared that Ali might be humiliated or seriously hurt if he took any other approach. Instead, Ali came out aggressively in the first round, taking the fight to Foreman with a series of dramatic right-hand leads. For the next six rounds, Ali executed the so-called 'rope-a-dope' manoeuvre by going to the ropes early in the round inviting Foreman to tire himself by throwing body punches, then attacking late in the round. Ali

Foreman falls after Ali's hard right

absorbed enormous punishment in the process. His strategy was nevertheless eventually effective. In the eighth round Ali knocked out an exhausted Foreman with a series of powerful combination punches. The fight and the lead up to it were perfectly captured in Leon Gast's 1996 documentary *When We Were Kings*.

The Open

10th - 13th July 1974 at Royal Lytham & St. Annes, Lancashire

Gary Player completed a hat-trick of Champion Golfer titles at Royal Lytham & St. Annes, having won his first Open at Muirfield in 1959 and his second at Carnoustie in 1968. With his triumph in 1974, he shared with Harry Vardon and J.H. Taylor the distinction of claiming the title in three separate decades. Fifteen years on from his first major win, he had added an eighth and was showing he still had an abundance of enthusiasm and dedication to produce his very best golf. He was the fourth player after Ben Hogan, Arnold Palmer and Jack Nicklaus to win the Masters and The Open in the same year. For the first time in The Open it was compulsory to play with the larger 1.68in ball, which had been used in America for many years and was less easy to control in the wind than the smaller ball. Inevitably, the wind blew on the first two days at Lytham.

Gary Player (pictured in 2008)

Player had an opening 69 to share the first-round lead with John Morgan and then moved ahead with a 68 on the second day. None of the other leading finishers broke 70 on either day. A 75 on the third day left Player still ahead of the field, with England's Peter Oosterhuis three behind. An eagle, three birdies and two bogeys in the first seven holes on the last day kept the chasing pack at bay, but Oosterhuis almost got back within one at the 13th, only for Player to chip in from the back of the green for a birdie. Player struggled with three bogeys in the last four holes. There was a long search for his ball in the rough at the 17th and he had to putt left-handed with his ball inches from the clubhouse wall at the last. However this gave him a 70 and a four-stroke win over Oosterhuis, with Jack Nicklaus pipping Hubert Green for fourth place thanks to a birdie at the last.

The USPGA

8th - 11th August 1974 at Tanglewood Park, Clemmons, North Carolina, USA

Lee Trevino fought off defending champ Jack Nicklaus in the final round, winning by one stroke over his rival. It was the fourth time Nicklaus finished second to Trevino in a major, and Trevino's fifth win in a major. Trevino led Nicklaus by one stroke after three rounds, having taken the tournament lead with a third-round 68 to Nicklaus' 70. Nicklaus battled Trevino all day in the final round, but in the end the two titans matched 69s and Trevino held onto his one-stroke advantage. The tournament featured two greats from a bygone era. In the 1938 tournament, which was then a matchplay, Paul Runyon beat Sam Snead 8&7 in the final. The two had mixed fortunes this time around. Runyon withdrew without completing the first round, but Snead opened with a 69, added back-to-back 71s in the middle rounds, and closed with a 68. His 279 total was three strokes shy of Trevino's winning total and tied 62-year-old Snead for third place.

With its revolutionary styling and scissor doors, the Lamborghini Countach LP400 first went on sale in 1974. Development was initiated by founder Ferruccio Lamborghini who was seeking a successor to the Miura. Marcello Gandini from Bertone designed the cars radical wedge look. The LP400's 3.9litre engine produced 370 horsepower.

The Volkswagen Golf Mk1 launched in 1974, marking a shift from VW's rear-engine, rear-wheel-drive Beetle to a front-engine, front-wheel-drive layout. Designed by Giorgetto Giugiaro, its angular, modern look became iconic. The Golf Mk1's practicality, reliability, and versatility quickly established it as a cornerstone of Volkswagen's lineup to this day.

The Panther De Ville, launched in 1974, was a luxury neo-classic car combining 1930s aesthetics with modern engineering. It featured a Jaguar engine, bespoke interiors, and a distinctive, elongated body. Of the 60 hand-built cars produced, owners included Elton John and Oliver Reed. The car was used as Cruella de Vil's car in the 2021 film Cruella.

Launched in 1974, the Citroën CX's futuristic design was packed with advanced technology, including hydropneumatic self-levelling suspension and self-centring steering. The interior featured a 'spaceship' style dashboard complete with revolving drum speedometer and tachometer. The car would go on to win the 1975 European Car of the Year award.

10 years after the launch of Nutella, the Ferrero company introduced the Kinder Surprise in 1974. The novel packaging combined a chocolate coated egg with a hidden toy inside. The idea was inspired by the Italian Easter tradition of giving children large chocolate eggs with toys inside. To date, over 30 billion Kinder Surprise eggs have been sold.

Contrary to popular belief, Skittles were created and first retailed in 1974 in the UK. The multicoloured fruit-flavoured lentil-shaped candies were originally marketed under the 'Galaxy' company logo. They are named after the sports game of the same name. Sales in the USA started in 1979. The 'Taste The Rainbow' slogan followed later in 1994.

Launched in 1974, Baileys Irish Cream was the first cream liqueur, blending Irish whiskey with cream and cocoa. Its formulation was partly inspired by the availability of alcohol from a money-losing distillery and surplus cream from a dairy increasingly producing semi-skimmed milk. The Baileys name was taken from a restaurant of the same name.

Skips crisps were launched in 1974 by KP Snacks in the UK. Known for their unique, fizzy, melt-in-the-mouth texture, Skips featured a distinctive prawn cocktail flavour. Their innovative production process creates light and airy crisps similar to Indonesian prawn crackers. They are made from tapioca starch in the UK and maize starch in Ireland.

The Rubik's Cube was invented in 1974 by Hungarian sculptor and professor of architecture Ernő Rubik. Originally named the 'Magic Cube', it has become the world's bestselling toy. With over 43 quintillion possible configurations, the world record for solving the 3x3x3 cube stands at 3.13 seconds, held by Max Park of the USA which he set in June 2023.

Playmobil was launched in 1974 by German toy maker Hans Beck for the Brandstätter Group. Featuring 7.5 cm figurines with movable parts, Playmobil sets encouraged imaginative play with themes like knights, pirates, and construction workers. As well as children, Playmobil has built a fan base of adult enthusiasts keen to own limited edition collectables.

Dungeons & Dragons (D&D), launched in 1974, was created by Gary Gygax and Dave Arneson. As the first tabletop role-playing game, it introduced players to immersive storytelling and character-driven adventures. Combining strategy and imagination, D&D revolutionised gaming, fostering a global community and influencing video games, books, and movies.

Connect 4 was launched in 1974 by Milton Bradley. Created by Howard Wexler and Ned Strongin, the game features a vertical grid where players drop coloured discs to align four in a row. Its simple rules and strategic depth has made Connect 4 an enduring classic. Interestingly, the first player can always win if they know to play a correct set of moves.

Photo Credits

Credits shown in the order in which they appear in the book. Photos not listed are in the public domain.

Key to page numbers

fc = front cover; **ifc** = inside front cover; **tp** = title page; **cp** = contents page; **ap1** = acknowledgements page 1; **ap2** = acknowledgements page 2; **ibc** = inside back cover; **bc** = back cover; **3** = page 3; **4** = page 4; etc.

Key to object position on page

tl = top left; *t* = top; *tc* = top centre; *tr* = top right; *cla* = centre left above; *ca* = centre above; *cra* = centre right above; *cl* = centre left; *c* = centre; *cr* = centre right; *clb* = centre left below; *cb* = centre below; *crb* = centre right below; *bl* = bottom left; *b* = bottom; *bc* = bottom centre; *br* = bottom right; *w* = whole page; *h* = header; *tb* = text background

Key to image licence types

CC BY-SA 2.0 = https://creativecommons.org/licenses/by-sa/2.0/deed.en; **CC BY-SA 3.0** = https://creativecommons.org/licenses/by-sa/3.0/deed.en; **CC BY-SA 4.0** = https://creativecommons.org/licenses/by-sa/4.0/deed.en; **(m)** = image modified (permitted by licensing terms)

fc *tc*: ABBA (m) © AVRO, Wikimedia Commons, CC BY-SA 3.0; **fc** *br*: John Lennon (m) © Tony Barnard, Los Angeles Times, Wikimedia Commons, CC BY-SA 4.0; **fc** *cla*: John Gielgud (m) © Allan Warren, Wikimedia Commons, CC BY-SA 3.0; **fc** *bl*: David Bowie (m) © AVRO, Wikimedia Commons, CC BY-SA 3.0; **tp** *w*: Lamborghini Countach (m) © Countachinfo.de, Wikimedia Commons, CC BY-SA 3.0; **2** *tr*: 10CC © AVRO, Wikimedia Commons, CC BY-SA 3.0; **3** *tl*: Sheila Young © Mieremet, Rob / Anefo, Wikimedia Commons, CC BY-SA 3.0; **3** *tc*: Teach In © AVRO, Wikimedia Commons, CC BY-SA 3.0; **4** *cla*: Princess Anne © Pelz, Wikimedia Commons, CC BY-SA 3.0; **5** *clb*: Lord Lucan © Trinity Mirror / Mirrorpix / Alamy Stock Photo; **16** *cla*: Melanie C © Raimond Spekking, Wikimedia Commons, CC BY-SA 4.0; **16** *clb*: Kate Moss © Renan Katayama, Wikimedia Commons, CC BY-SA 2.0; **17** *cla*: Christian Bale © Harald Krichel, Wikimedia Commons, CC BY-SA 4.0; **17** *clb*: Olivia Colman © Raph_PH, Wikimedia Commons, CC BY-SA 2.0; **18** *cla*: Robbie Williams © Drew de F Fawkes, Wikimedia Commons, CC BY-SA 2.0; **18** *clb*: James Blunt © Dani Dapena, Wikimedia Commons, CC BY-SA 2.0; **19** *cla*: Victoria Beckham © LGEPR, Wikimedia Commons, CC BY-SA 2.0; **19** *clb*: Penelope Cruz © Carlos Delgado, Wikimedia Commons, CC BY-SA 4.0; **20** *cla*: Tony McCoy © Sinn Féin, Wikimedia Commons, CC BY-SA 2.0; **20** *clb*: Jo Cox © with thanks to the Jo Cox Foundation; **21** *cla*: Maxine Peak © Brian Minkoff-London Pixels, Wikimedia Commons, CC BY-SA 4.0; **21** *clb*: Tim Henman © daramot, Wikimedia Commons, CC BY-SA 2.0; **22** *cla*: Gok Wan © Garry Knight, Wikimedia Commons, CC BY-SA 2.0; **22** *clb*: Leonardo DiCaprio © Presidencia de la República Mexicana, Wikimedia Commons, CC BY-SA 3.0; **23** *cla*: Paul Scholes © Christophe95, Wikimedia Commons, CC BY-SA 3.0; **23** *clb row 1*: Matt Lucas © Gage Skidmore, Wikimedia Commons, CC BY-SA 3.0; **23** *cb row 1*: Vaughan Gething © Senedd Cymru - Welsh Parliament, Wikimedia Commons, CC BY-SA 4.0; **23** *crb row 1*: Adil Ray © Adilray, Wikimedia Commons, CC BY-SA 3.0; **23** *clb row 2*: Andrea Corr © Tibor Pallerman, Wikimedia Commons, CC BY-SA 3.0; **23** *cb row 2*: Denise van Outen © Keven Law, Wikimedia Commons, CC BY-SA 2.0; **23** *crb row 2*: Alanis Morissette © Lunchbox LP, Wikimedia Commons, CC BY-SA 2.0; **23** *clb row 3*: Kelly Jones © RyAwesome, Wikimedia Commons, CC BY-SA 2.0; **23** *cb row 3*: Bear Grylls © Jamie Gray, Wikimedia Commons, CC BY-SA 2.0; **23** *crb row 3*: David Mitchell © Pinkboy, Wikimedia Commons, CC BY-SA 3.0; **23** *cb row 4*: Jimmy Fallon © Montclair Film Festival, Wikimedia Commons, CC BY-SA 2.0; **23** *crb row 4*: Matthew Macfadyen © Tomaholic, Wikimedia Commons, CC BY-SA 3.0; **23** *clb row 5*: Joaquin Phoenix © Harald Krichel, Wikimedia Commons, CC BY-SA 3.0; **23** *cb row 5*: Stephen Merchant © Carolyn Djanogly, Wikimedia Commons, CC BY-SA 2.0; **23** *crb row 5*: Sara Cox © Alex G, Wikimedia Commons, CC BY-SA 2.0; **24** *tl*: H.E. Bates © Pipplepop, Wikimedia Commons, CC BY-SA 4.0; **26** *tl*: Jo Smiley Hailey, Unsplash.com; **26** *cla*: Ford Cortina © Vauxford, Wikimedia Commons, CC BY-SA 4.0; **26** *tr*: House © Eric Lobel-Dunkley, Wikimedia Commons, CC BY-SA 2.0; **bl**: Sony Television © The Science Museum UK, Wikimedia Commons, CC BY-SA 4.0; **26** *bc*: Milk Bottles © Jason Murphy, Unsplash.com; **26** *br*: Petrol Station © Erik Mclean, Unsplash.com; **29** *br*: Space Hopper © Reptonix, Wikimedia Commons, CC BY-SA 3.0; **31** *tr*: Telephonist © FORTEPAN / Erky-Nagy Tibor, Wikimedia Commons, CC BY-SA 3.0; **32** *tl*: Bedroom wallpaper © purchase at www.baubauwall.com; **32** *bl*: Bathroom © Mike Shaw, Wikimedia Commons, CC BY-SA 4.0; **32** *crb*: Sunken Lounge © ♥threadbare on Flickr.com, CC BY-SA 2.0; **33** *tl*: Kitchen © AMCSviatko on Flickr.com, CC BY-SA 2.0; **33** *tr*: Peter Sellers © Allan Warren, Wikimedia Commons, CC BY-SA 3.0; **33** *bl*: Lava Lamp © Ryan Steele, Wikimedia Commons, CC BY-SA 4.0; **33** *crb*: Shag carpet © bradleyolin, Wikimedia Commons, CC BY-SA 2.0; **33** *br*: Shelf Drape © Auckland Museum, Wikimedia Commons, CC BY-SA 4.0; **34** *cra*: Chilli con carne © cyclonebill, Wikimedia Commons, CC BY-SA 2.0; **35** *c*: Sticky Toffee Pudding © Anton Diaz on Flickr.com, CC BY-SA 2.0; **36** *all images* © FORTEPAN / Schiffer Pál, Wikimedia Commons, CC BY-SA 3.0; **37** *tl*: Bell Bottoms © Mike Powell, Wikimedia Commons, CC BY-SA 3.0; **37** *tr*: Suzanna Leigh © Allan warren, Wikimedia Commons, CC BY-SA 3.0; **37** *bl*: Model in Trafalgar Square © FORTEPAN / Schiffer Pál, Wikimedia Commons, CC BY-SA 3.0; **37** *br*: Alan Bennett © Allan warren, Wikimedia Commons, CC BY-SA 3.0; **38** *tr*: Coach © Sludge G on Flickr.com, CC BY-SA 2.0; **38** *cl*: Sunbathing © Adományozó/Donor: Fortepan, Wikimedia Commons, CC BY-SA 3.0; **38** *br*: Ambleside © Peter Trimming, Wikimedia Commons, CC BY-SA 2.0; **39** *br*: Snowball Cocktail © Cheryl Morgan, Wikimedia Commons, CC BY-SA 4.0; **40** *br* **& 52** *tl* **& 53** *clb*: ABBA © AVRO, Wikimedia Commons, CC BY-SA 3.0; **41** *clb*: Walter Matthau © Everett Collection Inc / Alamy Stock Photo; **42** *cla*: Yellow Hotrod © Erwin Soo, Wikimedia Commons, CC BY-SA 2.0; **43** *clb*: Roger Moore © Allan warren, Wikimedia Commons, CC BY-SA 3.0; **44** *clb*: Boat and Island © David Dixon, Geograph.org.uk, CC BY-SA 2.0; **46** *clb*: Ronnie Barker © PA Images / Alamy Stock Photo; **47** *cla*: Mr.Men book © True Images / Alamy Stock Photo; **47** *clb*: Rising Damp © Allstar Picture Library Limited. / Alamy Stock Photo; **48** *clb*: Tom's Midnight Garden image created with the assistance of DALL·E 3; **49** *cra*: Roger Day (m) © Acabashi, Wikimedia Commons, CC BY-SA 4.0; **50** *bl*: Leonard Cohen © Gorupdebesanez, Wikimedia Commons, CC BY-SA 3.0; **51** *tl*: Wings © Corwin~commonswiki, Wikimedia Commons, CC BY-SA 4.0; **51** *bl* **& 53** *crb*: David Essex © Margaret Morley, Wikimedia Commons, CC BY-SA 2.0; **53** *various*: Slade / Mud / Suzi Quatro / Alvin Stardust / Paper Lace © AVRO, Wikimedia Commons, CC BY-SA 3.0; **53** *cla*: The New Seekers © Nationaal Archief, Den Haag, Rijksfotoarchief, Wikimedia Commons, CC BY-SA 3.0; **53** *bl*: Ray Stevens © Gene Pugh, Wikimedia Commons, CC BY-SA 2.0; **53** *cra*: George McCrae © MiamiFilmFestival, Wikimedia Commons, CC BY-SA 2.0; **54** *tr*: Marina Abramović © Francesco Pierantoni, Wikimedia Commons, CC BY-SA 2.0; **54** *cl*: World Cup © Marcello Casal JR/ABr, Wikimedia Commons, CC BY-SA 3.0; **55-57** All images except President Nixon (*bl* p56) created with the assistance of DALL·E 3/ Adobe Photoshop; **58** *clb*: Tom Stoppard © Gorup de Besanez, Wikimedia Commons, CC BY-SA 3.0; **59** *tl*: Terry Gilliam © Eduardo Unda-Sanzana, Wikimedia Commons, CC BY-SA 2.0; **59** *clb*: Bernard Hill © Gemma Longman, Wikimedia Commons, CC BY-SA 2.0; **60** *tl*: Goslar Warrior © Koppchen, Wikimedia Commons, CC BY-SA 3.0; **60** *tr*: Henry Moore © Allan warren, Wikimedia Commons, CC BY-SA 3.0; **60** *bl*: Four Lads sculpture © Spaz Tacular, Wikimedia Commons, CC BY-SA 2.0; **60** *br*: Arthur Dooley © writingonthewall.org.uk; **61** *cl*: St Mary Magdalene Church © DeFacto, Wikimedia Commons, CC BY-SA 4.0; **61** *bl*: St Michael and All Angels © John Salmon, Wikimedia Commons, CC BY-SA 2.0; *continued on next page...*

Photo credits continued... **62** *tr*: Black Hole © EHT Collaboration, Wikimedia Commons, CC BY-SA 4.0; **62** *bl*: Arecibo msg © Arne Nordmann, Wikimedia Commons, CC BY-SA 3.0; **66** *clb*: Squirrel helicopter © ComensoliDavide, Wikimedia Commons, CC BY-SA 4.0; **68** *tr* & *cl*: Terracotta Army © xiquinhosilva, Wikimedia Commons, CC BY-SA 2.0; **69** *cl* & *br*: Damaged houses © Billbeee, Wikimedia Commons, CC BY-SA 3.0; **70** *tr*: Lord Lucan © Trinity Mirror / Mirrorpix / Alamy Stock Photo; **72** *tr*: John Stonehouse © André Cros, Wikimedia Commons, CC BY-SA 4.0; **73** *clb*: Senate hearing © Senate photographer, Wikimedia Commons, CC BY-SA 3.0; **74** *bl*: Limo © Barabbas1312, Wikimedia Commons, CC BY-SA 4.0; **75** *br*: Escort to courthouse © John Malmin, Los Angeles Times, Wikimedia Commons, CC BY-SA 4.0; **77** *tr*: Jimmy Connors © Koen Suyk / Anefo, Wikimedia Commons, CC BY-SA 4.0; **78** *tr*: Gordon Brown © Robyburns, Wikimedia Commons, CC BY-SA 4.0; **79** *tr*: Lillee and Thomson © PA Images / Alamy Stock Photo; **80** *tr*: Red Rum © Keystone Press / Alamy Stock Photo; **84** *t*: Countach (m) © Countachinfo.de, Wikimedia Commons, CC BY-SA 3.0; **84** *b*: VW Golf Mk 1 (m) © Maxim Kukurund/stock.adobe.com; **85** *t*: Panther de Ville (m) © Mr.choppers, Wikimedia Commons, CC BY-SA 3.0; **85** *b*: Citroen CX (m) © KlausNahr, Wikimedia Commons, CC BY-SA 2.0; **86** *t*: Kinder Surprise (m) © AlenKadr/Walter Cicchetti/stock.adobe.com; **86** *b*: Skittles (m) © PhotoEdit/rvlsoft/stock.adobe.com; **87** *t*: Baileys (m) © mehaniq41/stock.adobe.com; **87** *b*: Skips (m) © lenscap50/Monkey Business/stock.adobe.com; **88** *t*: Rubiks Cube (m) © wachiwit/stock.adobe.com; **88** *b*: Playmobil (m) © AUFORT Jérome/stock.adobe.com; **89** *t*: D&D (m) © Esther/stock.adobe.com; **89** *b*: Connect 4 (m) © Ana Belen Garcia/stock.adobe.com; **92** *tc*: Coffee Table (m) © Sincerely Media, Unsplash.com; **BC** *cla*: Queen Elizabeth (m) © Archives New Zealand, Wikimedia Commons, CC BY-SA 2.0; **BC** *tc*: Lee Remick (m) © Allan Warren, Wikimedia Commons, CC BY-SA 3.0;

Graphic and Background Image Credits

Credits shown in the order in which they appear in the book.

Additional Key (ic) = icon; (ph) = photo

fc *c*, **tp** *ca* & **bc**: (ph) Texture (m) © Felipe Santana, unsplash.com; **2-15**: (ph) Wood (m) © Michael Schwarzenberger, pixabay.com; **2-3, 16-91** *tb*: (ph) Paper Texture (m) © rawpixel.com; **3** *cla*: (ic) Play (m) © Adrien Coquet, thenounproject.com, CC BY-SA 3.0; **6,8,10,12,14** *tl* & **7,9,11,13,15** *tr*: (ic) Newspaper (m) © Loic Poivet, thenounproject.com, CC BY-SA 3.0; **6-15** *c*: (ph) Book (m) © Robert Armstrong, pixabay.com; **16,18,20,22** *tr* & **17,19,21,23** *tr*: (ic) Birthday Calendar (m) © Kiran Shastry, thenounproject.com, CC BY-SA 3.0; **16-25, 40-61, 84-92** *w*: (m)(ph) Concrete Terrazzo Wall (m) © rawpixel.com; **16,18,19** *cla* & **18** *clb*: (ic) Microphone (m) © andriwidodo, thenounproject.com, CC BY-SA 3.0; **16** *clb* (ic) Mannequin (m) © Blair Adams, thenounproject.com, CC BY-SA 3.0; **17** *cla* & **19,22** *clb*: (ic) Clapper Board (m) © Andrew Nielsen, thenounproject.com, CC BY-SA 3.0; **17** *clb* & **21** *cla* (ic) Theatre (m) © Ben Davis, thenounproject.com, CC BY-SA 3.0; **20** *cla*: (ic) Jocket (m) Road Signs, thenounproject.com, CC BY-SA 3.0; **20,24** *clb*: (ic) Speaker (m) © popcornarts, thenounproject.com, CC BY-SA 3.0; **21** *clb*: (ic) Tennis (m) © Musmellow, thenounproject.com, CC BY-SA 3.0; **22** *cla*: (ic) Television (m) © Adrien Coquet, thenounproject.com, CC BY-SA 3.0; **23** *cla*: (ic) Football (m) © leo-graph.com, thenounproject.com, CC BY-SA 3.0; **23** *clb*: (ic) Baby (m) © Emily Keller, thenounproject.com, CC BY-SA 3.0; **24** *tl* & **25** *tr*: (ic) Wreath (m) © Alex Muravev, thenounproject.com, CC BY-SA 3.0; **24** *cla*: (ic) Book (m) © Travis Avery, thenounproject.com, CC BY-SA 3.0; **24** *cl*: (ic) Music Note (m) © karen tyler, thenounproject.com, CC BY-SA 3.0; **25** *clb*: (ic) Music Note (m) © karen tyler, thenounproject.com, CC BY-SA 3.0; **25** *cla*: (ic) Army (m) © ahmad, thenounproject.com, CC BY-SA 3.0; **25** *cl*: (ic) Nuclear (m) © Ricons, thenounproject.com, CC BY-SA 3.0; **25** *clb*: (ic) Theatre Comedy (m) © b farias, thenounproject.com, CC BY-SA 3.0; **26-38** *w*: (m)(ph) White Concrete Wall (m) © rawpixel.com; **26** *tl*: (ic) Coins (m) © Evgenii Likhachov, thenounproject.com, CC BY-SA 3.0; **27** (ic) School Desk (m) © Jongrak, thenounproject.com, CC BY-SA 3.0; **28** *tl*: (ic) Exams (m) © Arjan Farzkenari, thenounproject.com, CC BY-SA 3.0; **29** *tr*: (ic) Children (m) © IronSV, thenounproject.com, CC BY-SA 3.0; **30** *tl*: (ic) Mine (m) © Vectors Market, thenounproject.com, CC BY-SA 3.0; **31** *tr*: (ic) Office (m) © Anggara Putra, thenounproject.com, CC BY-SA 3.0; **32** *tl* & **33** *tr*: (ic) Home (m) © Numero Uno, thenounproject.com, CC BY-SA 3.0; **34** *tl*: (ic) Chili (m) © Mello, thenounproject.com, CC BY-SA 3.0; **35** *tr*: (ic) Pudding (m) © Ranah Pixel Studio, thenounproject.com, CC BY-SA 3.0; **36** *tl* & **37** *tr*: (ic) Fashion (m) © Mahmure Alp, thenounproject.com, CC BY-SA 3.0; **38** *tl*: (ic) Holiday (m) © Claudia Revalina, thenounproject.com, CC BY-SA 3.0; **39** *tr*: (ic) Christmas Tree (m) © Azam Ishaq, thenounproject.com, CC BY-SA 3.0; **39** *w*: Christmas (m) © Annie Spratt, unsplash.com; **40** *tl*: (ic) Entertainment (m) © shashank singh, thenounproject.com, CC BY-SA 3.0; **41,43** *tr* & **42,44** *tl*: (ic) Clapper Board (m) © Andrew Nielsen, thenounproject.com, CC BY-SA 3.0; **45** *tl*: (ic) Award (m) © Carlos von Dessauer, thenounproject.com, CC BY-SA 3.0; **46,48** *tl* & **47** *tr*: (ic) Television (m) © Adrien Coquet, thenounproject.com, CC BY-SA 3.0; **49** *tr*: (ic) Radio (m) © GreenHill, thenounproject.com, CC BY-SA 3.0; **50,52** *tl* & **51** *tr*: (ic) Record (m) © Mourad Mokrane, thenounproject.com, CC BY-SA 3.0; **53** *tr*: (ic) Music Note (m) © karen tyler, thenounproject.com, CC BY-SA 3.0; **54** *tl*: (ic) Arts (m) © Kelsey Armstrong, thenounproject.com, CC BY-SA 3.0; **55,57** *tr* & **56** *tl*: (ic) Book (m) © Travis Avery, thenounproject.com, CC BY-SA 3.0; **58** *tl* & **59** *tr* (ic) Theatre (m) © Ben Davis, thenounproject.com, CC BY-SA 3.0; **60** *tl*: (ic) Sculpture (m) © Creative Mania, thenounproject.com, CC BY-SA 3.0; **61** *tr*: (ic) Poetry (m) © Martin, thenounproject.com, CC BY-SA 3.0; **62-67** *w*: (ph) Plasma (m) © Hal Gatewood, unsplash.com; **62** *tl* & **63** *tr*: (ic) Space (m) © Trevor Dsouza, thenounproject.com, CC BY-SA 3.0; **64** *tl*: (ic) Fair (m) © Amethyst Studio, thenounproject.com, CC BY-SA 3.0; **65** *tr*: (ic) Old Computer (m) © Juicy Fish, thenounproject.com, CC BY-SA 3.0; **66** *tl* & **67** *tr*: (ic) Fighter Jet (m) © Nico Ilk, thenounproject.com, CC BY-SA 3.0; **68** *tl*: (ic) Army (m) © Maxicons, thenounproject.com, CC BY-SA 3.0; **68** *w*: (ph) Terracotta Army (m) © xiquinhosilva, Wikimedia Commons, CC BY-SA 2.0; **69** *tr*: (ic) Tornado (m) © Aquariid, thenounproject.com, CC BY-SA 3.0; **69** *w*: (ph) Tornado (m) © Nikolas Noonan, unsplash.com; **70** *tl*: (ic) Missing (m) © Fran Couto, thenounproject.com, CC BY-SA 3.0; **70** *w*: (ph) Road (m) © benjamin lehman, unsplash.com; **71** *tr*: (ic) Escape (m) © Adrien Coquet, thenounproject.com, CC BY-SA 3.0; **71** *w*: (ph) Ghetto (m) © Austrian National Library, unsplash.com; **72** *tl*: (ic) Spy (m) © H Alberto Gongora, thenounproject.com, CC BY-SA 3.0; **72** *w*: (ph) Beach (m) © Roland Denes, unsplash.com; **73** *tr*: (ic) Security Breach (m) © Saishraddha Malage, thenounproject.com, CC BY-SA 3.0; **74** *tl*: (ic) Princess (m) © Circlon Tech, thenounproject.com, CC BY-SA 3.0; **74** *w*: (ph) The Mall (m) © Fran The Now Time, unsplash.com; **75** *tr*: (ic) Gang (m) © Alina Oleynik, thenounproject.com, CC BY-SA 3.0; **75** *w*: (ph) Dollars (m) © Dmytro Demidko, unsplash.com; **76** *tl*: (ic) Football (m) © leo-graph.com, thenounproject.com, CC BY-SA 3.0; **76** *w*: (ph) Football Pitch (m) © Alberto Frías, unsplash.com; **77** *tr*: (ic) Tennis (m) © Mister Pixel, thenounproject.com, CC BY-SA 3.0; **77** *w*: (ph) Tennis Court (m) © Max Zindel, unsplash.com; **78** *tl*: (ic) Rugby Ball (m) © Marco Livolsi, thenounproject.com, CC BY-SA 3.0; **78** *w*: (ph) Rugby Match (m) © Alex Motoc, unsplash.com; **78** *h*: (ph) Rugby Lineout (m) © Auckland Museum, Wikimedia Commons, CC BY-SA 4.0; **79** *tr*: (ic) Cricket (m) © Bernd Lakenbrink, thenounproject.com, CC BY-SA 3.0; **79** *w*: (ph) Cricketer (m) © Yogendra Singh, unsplash.com; **80** *tl*: (ic) Horse Racing (m) © Sergio Morozov, thenounproject.com, CC BY-SA 3.0; **80** *w*: (ph) Racehorse (m) © Luisa Peter, unsplash.com; **80** *h*: (ph) Horse Race © Jongsun Lee, Wikimedia Commons, CC BY-SA 3.0; **81** *tr*: (ic) Race Car (m) © Slidicon, thenounproject.com, CC BY-SA 3.0; **81** *w*: (ph) Chequered Flag (m) © Bas van den Eijkhof, unsplash.com; **81** *h*: (ph) Old Race Car (m) © Jeff Cooper, unsplash.com; **82** *tl*: (ic) Boxing Glove (m) © Anton Anuchin, thenounproject.com, CC BY-SA 3.0; **82** *w*: (ph) Boxing Match (m) © Johann Walter Bantz, unsplash.com; **83** *tr*: (ic) Golfer (m) © Nicolas Vicent, thenounproject.com, CC BY-SA 3.0; **83** *w*: (ph) Golfing (m) © Courtney Cook, unsplash.com; **83** *h*: (ph) Golf Ball (m) © mk. s, unsplash.com; **84,86,88** *tl* & **85,87,89** *tr*: (ic) Framed Picture (m) © Lil Squid, thenounproject.com, CC BY-SA 3.0; **90** *tl* & **91** *tr*: (ic) Camera (m) © AomAm, thenounproject.com, CC BY-SA 3.0; **92** *tl*: (ic) Present (m) © Vinzence Studio, thenounproject.com, CC BY-SA 3.0

1974 : What A Year To Be Born!
Why not join our mailing list...

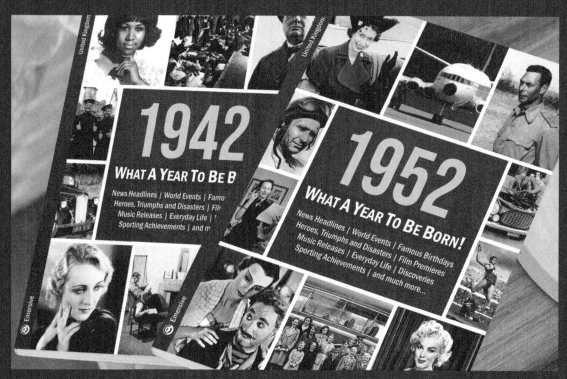

Join us for news on our future releases, reader promotions and behind-the-scenes content. All at:

www.subscribepage.com/whatayear

It's completely free to join. As a subscriber, we will email you no more than once or twice a month.
We will never share your email address and you can unsubscribe at any time.

Answers to the Eleven-plus Exam on page 28

Arithmetic Questions

Q1: London to Birmingham is 120 miles
Q2: Christmas Day will fall on a Thursday
Q3: It will take 6 hours and 40 minutes
Q4: Five hundred and twenty three
Q5: A) John's mother was 40 years old
Q5: B) In 3 years' time
Q5: C) John will be 30 years old

General English Questions

Q1: A) Our dogs are carrying sticks.
Q1: B) Their butchers have no meat.
Q1: C) Men who like football are sure to have team scarves in their houses.
Q2: A) Finger
Q2: B) Umpire
Q2: C) Spaniards
Q3: A) Certain or sure
Q3: B) Shortly or soon
Q3: C) Decided

Printed in Great Britain
by Amazon

47893119R00053